movement
training
for actors

JACKIE SNOW

methuen | drama

Methuen Drama

1 3 5 7 9 10 8 6 4 2

First published in 2012

Methuen Drama, an imprint of Bloomsbury Publishing Plc

Methuen Drama
Bloomsbury Publishing Plc
50 Bedford Square
London WC1B 3DP
www.methuendrama.com

ISBN: 978 1 408 12857 2

A CIP catalogue record for this book is available from the British Library

Available in the USA from
Bloomsbury Academic & Professional
175 Fifth Avenue/3rd Floor
New York
NY 10010.

Typeset by Margaret Brain
Printed and bound in Great Britain by CPI Group (UK) Ltd, Croydon CR0 4YY

For my Parents, Alison and David and my boys: Sean, Liam and Christie

Acknowledgements

I would like to thank, Sue Lefton, for introducing me to movement training for actors nearly thirty years ago, and her on-going teaching, wisdom and mentoring since. I would also like to thank Trish Arnold, who, in her 93rd year is still as enthusiastic about movement for actors, in particular the swings, and who taught me in such detail then, and still manages to inspire and infuse my teaching with new thought and energy.

I would also like to thank all my colleagues at the Guildhall School of Music and Drama, in particular Wendy Allnutt, with whom I have worked side by side for nearly thirty years, and with whom I consolidated this version of movement training by daily teaching, conversation and practice. To Terry Worrall, for his music and historical expertise; to Ian Wooldridge, BADA, and Wyn Jones, Guildhall, whose insights into directing were so wholeheartedly inclusive of movement, that it enabled me to translate the work that was done in the studio, to a play, and so taught me about movement direction. To Patsy Rodenburg, Jeanette Nelson and Charmian Hoare, for their wisdom in understanding the need for movement to support the voice.

I would like to acknowledge the following for their contribution to this work, and who, although we all have our own individual approaches to it, our one thing in common is Trish Arnold and Pure Movement: Jane Gibson, Shona Morris, Danny McGrath, Elizabeth Ballinger, Jack Murphy and Merry Conway.

I would also like to thank the following colleagues and friends, who have contributed to the book and for endless conversation and support; Jenny Hollier, Carolyn Sands, and all my colleagues at the British American Drama Academy; Catherine Charlton, Michael Gaunt, Niamh Dowling, Madeleine Potter, Richard Ryan, Mick Barnfather, Marcelle Davies, Clive Rowe, Ellen Newman, Robert Price, Deborah Gray and Yu Xin from the Central Academy of Drama, Beijing.

I thank and acknowledge the contribution and expertise of the staff at the Royal Academy of Dramatic Art, which has culminated in the writing of this book.

Thanks to the following RADA students for participating in filming the DVD and photographs, and for Peter Todd in making it. Hiran Abeysekera; Shanaya Rafaat; Eline Pauwels; Jordan Mifsud; Imogen Daines; Scarlet Brookes; Daisy Hughes; Molly Logan and Kiza Deen.

A warm thank you to Maryanne Nicholls for allowing us to use her art work for the front cover of the book, and everyone at Methuen: Jenny Ridout, Charlotte Loveridge, Judy Tither and Kim Muranyi .To Victoria Ross for being the first person to read it through and commenting on it so helpfully and Keith Pusey for his endless support and patience.

And finally a special thanks to my family and all the students I have ever taught.

Contents

Preface

First encounters with movement training

When young actors arrive at drama school they are confronted with an array of technical classes that will underpin their three years' vocational training. Drama schools normally draw up a philosophical statement that sets out a school's mission, training aims and outcomes, and describes in outline the type of actor expected to emerge at the end of the training period.

During the early stages, of course, cohorts engage with basic techniques in acting, voice production and movement, as they study and progress their basic performance skills: public performances will come later once techniques become proficient. This initial focus on the development of techniques and skills will usually pre-dominate, especially in the first year of training, as the actors learn to engage imaginatively with the study of texts and scenes abstracted from a range of plays. Parallel with this work, actors will learn how vocal and physical skills help to support and reveal characterisations and narratives.

Heads of departments and senior teachers with responsibility for the delivery of acting, voice and movement classes will work together to plan a syllabus in keeping with a school's philosophy that supports the holistic and progressive development of their students. As the training period proceeds and the actors enter their second and third years of training the balance within a syllabus will change as techniques and skills develop in readiness for the demands and challenges of final year performances, both on stage and for the camera lens.

Movement forms an intrinsic and essential part of an actor's training and will incorporate a range of classes and exercises that will enable an actor to develop physical confidence, suppleness, strength and, in due course, physical presence. Importantly, he or she, will come to recognise that the body is the actor's instrument. Like a musical instrument it has to be cared for, maintained, exercised and energised for performance; it has to be tuned and ready (as does the voice) for the exact moment of performance. Unlike a musical instrument it cannot be put away in a case until it is next needed and tuned prior to the next performance: nor can it be replaced!

Just as each actor is different, so is each character and one of the great pleasures of acting is to discover these differences as the play is studied and rehearsed, and a character's place and dramatic function within the action is understood and prepared for performance. The value of physical warm-up sessions will be experienced, and as training progresses these sessions will allow the actors to explore, through awareness of their own bodies, the physical characteristics pertinent to each role they play. Period movement and dance will further enhance an actor's preparation and awareness of differences in style. During their research and preparation actors will become sympathetic to the period in which a character may have lived, or is living, and the character's status within that society; they will have an understanding of a character's faith and fears, they will come to identify prevailing manners, or the lack of them, and how people greeted each other; they will investigate prevalent social life and pastimes – eighteenth century fashionable balls, country dancing and contrast these with a present day night club life and its codes of behaviour; they will notice a character's native intelligence; they will see the clothing a character has selected to wear and how movement is affected by fashion. The actor will understand how clothing will indicate a character's status or profession and its impact on movement and mobility: the list is endless. Each play can offer the actor a cluster of creative opportunities which enable him or her to bring a character to 'life' within 'the world of the play' through the exploration of physicality and movement.

There are many teachers and many approaches to an actor's physical training. A question that should be answered is how an actor's training supports him or her in the search for employment in the present day profession? What use is movement or dance to an actor? How can it be employed to support and enrich the actor's training? These are searching questions and there is not space here to address them. But here an example of the usefulness of a physical acting exercise can be considered. Take a series of silent improvisation that can used to explore a character's mental and emotional state and how ensuing changes are evident in a character's physicality and attitude when there is a sudden and unexpected shift of circumstances:

The character enters a room and takes a key from a hook without any difficulty, that is, there are no obstacles as the key is where it should be: the character takes it and leaves the room.

The character enters a room. This time there is a change in the circumstances as she is late, she has overslept and is in danger of being late to meet friends. The key is not where it should be. There is an obstacle – the key is missing.

This is not a major obstacle, but there might be a noticeable change in the character's physical rhythm and emotional state while the key is sought. The physical rhythm will change again when the key is found and the character leaves the room.

The character enters a room and is unable to find a key. The circumstances are more complicated because this is the morning of an important job interview and the character has been unemployed for a long period. The missing key is a serious obstacle to face and the character's emotional and physical state changes and the tempo of the search increases, as the character fails to find the key: there is dramatic tension. When the key is found in a pocket, or a handbag with a ripped lining, changes in rhythm and tempo takes place and the scene's atmosphere changes, the tension reduces as the character leaves the room.

The character enters a room quickly. A key cannot be found. Where is it?
A visitor to the house has fallen down stairs and is unconscious, there is blood: he must be driven at once to the hospital. The action is frantic. Where is the car key? The tension increases as the search continues: this could be a matter of life and death! The key is found. The tension reduces the character experiences relief. The atmosphere is charged as the character leaves in haste.

In the above exercises the character's intention each time is to find the key and her actions are conditioned by changes in the circumstances. Significantly, through the medium of the actor, narrative and dramatic tension are revealed through a character's physicality, as he or she lives through a set of changing circumstances, confronts obstacles and then overcomes then: not a word is needed to communicate the narrative.

Once actors engage in their final year of training, if they are lucky, they will meet characters from a variety of play genre. These might include characters caught up in Pinter's comedy of menace, or those to be found in Rattigan's world of sensitively observed upper class characters. If they are really lucky the actors might enter the robustly physical eighteenth century world of *The Rivals* by R. B. Sheridan. The play begins with the servant Fag and the coachman, who have just arrived in separate coaches in Bath, discussing the characters with whom they have travelled and who will shortly appear in the play. The audience hears about Mrs Malaprop, one of the great comedic characters in the English play repertoire, and Sir Anthony Absolute, both of whom suffer from stiff joints and in Sir Anthony's case he is also a victim of gout. Jack Absolute, his adventurous son, is in the army and is trained to use the sword he carries. When he is challenged to a duel his reluctant challenger can barely hold a loaded pistol. Jack, under an assumed name, and Mrs Malaprop's niece, Lydia, make love to each other according to eighteenth century etiquette and manners. The numerous physical actions that abound in the play support the flow and fun of the action: they are 'real' to the characters and in this lies much of the play's humour. An audience's response and laughter grows out of each character's predicament as they earnestly attempt to resolve matters: if there is no physical characterisation to support the action, then there is no play.

The teaching of movement for actors has become increasingly important today when members of society generally do not exercise regularly and walk less than previous generations. Many of today's young people spend long hours on computers, iPods and mobile phones and are not always physically fit and agile: actors need to be fit and agile and a sound introduction to movement and how it supports characterisation will be of benefit to them throughout their professional lives. It will be evident to the reader that Jackie Snow is a movement teacher rich in knowledge and practical experience. Her years of teaching have been balanced with prestigious movement work and direction in London's West End theatres, leading regional theatres and international movies.

In her writing Jackie Snow sets out a wealth of information and advice to encourage movement teachers who are committed to training the next generation of actors. And, of course, if they glance at the book it will remind present day actors of the valuable movement training they received at drama school.

Professor Michael Gaunt
Former actor, and past principal the Guildford School
of Acting and Birmingham School of Acting

Introduction

Why the actor's body needs training

'I think movement can be one of the hardest parts of training for an actor. Musicians, dancers, singers and painters do not have this problem because they must first achieve a specific level of technical ability before they can progress to their full potential. Acting is an amorphous art and TV gives the young aspirant the idea that if one is "natural" that is all that is needed. Actually no acting is natural. I believe that to appear "natural" the actor has to give up some of the habits that he has accumulated. For example, they may have always stood with locked knees or drooping shoulders. This posture is hard to change because what is habitual is safe. But he/she must unlock his/her expressive imaginative body.

If one compares a play with a symphony, you can say that the actor is both the instrumentalist and the instrument. He is an instrumentalist because he translates, through the use of his intelligence, sensibility, and artistry, a written text, just as a musician translates a written score. He is an instrument because he can express his art with his voice and the movement of his body.'

TRISH ARNOLD

The intention of this book is to describe what has become known as 'Movement for Actors'. It is a description of the approach to one aspect of the training of actors at the Royal Academy of Dramatic Art (RADA) and many other drama schools. The philosophy behind the movement training is to train the students to become as versatile actors as possible. The aim for the trained actor is to have at their disposal the techniques which will allow them to achieve the greatest or smallest physical and imaginative transformation. They should have the technical ability to work in the largest theatres of the world or on film and television; they should be able to perform in musical theatre or physical theatre; they should have the physical control required to work on the radio. Bearing in mind the thinking behind this aspect of the trainee actor's work I will outline many of the exercises and games I have used both at RADA, the Guildhall School of Music and Drama (GSMD), and also at other actor educational establishments, in particular the British American Drama Academy (BADA). It is appreciated that 'Movement for Actors' has evolved from a vast range of sources and many of those teachers and students who have contributed to the present thinking about this topic are mentioned in the appendix.

Of all the facets of drama training, perhaps the most difficult to teach through the medium of the page is movement. After all, very little about this discipline is about verbal communication or instruction. Trainee actors need to come to a full understanding of the way his/her body moves. That can only be accomplished by standing up, following exercises, discussing the results and experimenting with the capabilities and shortcomings of their bodies.

There are many disciplines that are based on physical expression; body awareness and alignment, mask work, clowning and circus skills, physical characterisation, spatial relationships, ensemble work, improvisation, games, mime and expressive acrobatics, to name a few.

The DVD and photographs that accompany this book, therefore, are visual guides to aid the understanding, learning and development of the reader.

What is *not* movement training for an actor?

Yoga, Pilates, tai chi, capoeira, gymnastics, ballet and other forms of formal dance and martial art are not considered movement training for the actor. They are all good methods of fitness and body training but, despite having a performance component, do not lead to the physical expression of a dramatic action or imaginative idea, as the actor movement training does.

A brief history of this method of movement training for actors

Movement for actors, as it is now understood and taught at many major drama schools, is an amalgamation of many practitioners (see appendix) brought together through Litz Pisk and Trish Arnold, the legendary British movement teacher and collaborator of Kristin Linklater (voice teacher), who works on marrying this movement to work with the voice, using the movement work to free the body for the voice. Trish was trained by Sigurd Leeder of the Kurt Joss ballet, who was also a long time collaborator of Rudolph Laban. Both Litz and Trish infused Joss's release-based swings with breath work specifically for actors and used Laban's dimensions and use of movement qualities. She was particularly influenced by Jacques Lecoq's mask work, the neutral and character mask, animals and elements and dramatic acrobatics. She also incorporated some of Jerzy Grotowski's work, in particular The Cat. The Feldenkrais and F.M. Alexander principles are used for body alignment and efficient usage of the body. Period dance is also used for rhythm and style, elegance and deportment, relationship with the space and the spatial relationships between people, for example status relationships which includes what kind of space to put between people, and manner of characters in plays. It was developed for actors through Belinda Quirey's work, where the ultimate goal was for the work to create the illusion of real people who danced, and not a plastic art, as in other formal dance methods. The work evolves from research, history, and imagination, which is then expressed and explored through the movement. That period character, like all other characters, cannot be stuck on like an outer layer but must evolve from a place of truth and reality .

The purposes of movement training

Firstly, this kind of movement work loosens and strengthens the body, and provides the actor with specialist skills to perform. There are examples of this throughout the book.

Secondly, it develops ways of expressing thought and imagination, allowing actors to create characters from the inside-out or outside-in, and helps them to manifest the inner workings of the mind through the body. The end result should be that the actor gains the control of their body in order to use it exactly in the way that they want to. Actors need to have at their disposal an instrument which, at all times, expresses their dramatic intention. The actor's training is similar to that of a musician practising with an instrument, to gain the best possible skills, it is fine-tuning the body – and the voice – to enable the actor to achieve the highest level of expressiveness in their art.

Thirdly, the movement work educates the actor in ways of working with a director to explore the physicality of character and text without interfering with their vision for the play.

Although this book will look at some of these things, the reader should bear in mind that this is not a syllabus, but an approach to training. The exercises on a practical level aim to release excess tension and allow the body to work efficiently with ease to support the breath and consequently the voice. Additionally, they aim to open the door to an awareness of the possibilities of using the body when preparing for characterisation.

So, the first priority in a movement lesson is to release tension and free the breath. Only then will it be possible for the actor's imagination and invention to be matched by the ability to express through the body and voice.

People can get the idea, from watching naturalistic performances in films and television programmes, that 'acting natural' is all that is needed. Acting involves creating the illusion of life on the stage or for the lens: it is far from 'natural'. Indeed, actors have to begin by giving up some of the 'natural' habits that they have accumulated. They do not need to give up every habit because, often, some of the habits are what keep the actor's own individuality. The main craft of an actor is to be able to transform themselves, and it takes a lot of practice and discipline to achieve transformation – or indeed, just to look 'natural'. Think of ballet dancers who undergo decades of the most rigorous training possible in order to give the appearance of floating like a butterfly. Although the ballet dancers appear to float like a butterfly, they feel sore, aching and exhausted. How the performer feels does not necessarily translate to the audience.

Attaining a 'natural' or 'effortless' quality means taking risks and breaking down habits. For example, if the actor has always stood with a displaced spine, a collapsed chest and a poking neck, locked knees and drooping shoulders, it can be hard to change. Similarly, if the actor has experienced vigorous training (for example, in ballet or rugby) it can be difficult to lose the physical traits and usage associated with that training. In fact, losing these habits can be emotionally painful because most postural habits, whether they are the results of ballet, bodybuilding, football training, help us to feel safe and link to our sense of identity. Not every character the actor plays is going to have the same physicality. Shedding some of those old habits can also be liberating and exciting, particularly as the actor learns new techniques and begins to see what their body can do. The aim is to find your expressive natural body. In training actors we are not aiming to turn anyone into Arnold Schwarzenegger or Chris Hoy. What we are working towards is eliminating the gap between the thought and the movement, making the body as free, strong and flexible as possible.

When you see a 'straight' text-based play, there is often little attention given to posture and movement, resulting in actors having physicality very similar to that of their own, and voices which are shouting out of tense, locked bodies with poking necks. The potential problem for an untrained actor is that they may need to shout to be heard, due to bad posture, leaning forward from the waist, straining their necks, and using unwanted tension to indicate passion.

Movement training should train the actor in the same way that a performer tunes a musical instrument. Once they have become a finely tuned instrument, they should then be capable of noticing the subtle phases of perception and intention, in relation to characterisation. An actor who is comfortable both in stillness and in activity, who commits to both, and who moves easily from one state to another is an actor who commands the stage. Training in movement provides a way for the teacher and student to grasp and hold on to the intangible concept called 'presence'.

Movement training works in two specific ways. Firstly, on a practical level, the actor can release excess tension in the body, and allow it to work efficiently with ease, whilst being able to support the breath and consequently the voice. Secondly, as Trish Arnold says, to 'open a door to an awareness of the possibilities in using the body' and through this to discover the freedom and intensity of expression an actor requires to communicate and reach their audience.

The training helps actors to develop their instrument in a primary way, creating a basic understanding of the relationship with space, time, weight, gravity and impulse. Actors also need to become a sound vessel to absorb and project the thoughts and imagination of the playwright and/or the director.

So teaching movement for actors involves working with the trainee actors' bodies, using the technique which, though based on history, is being continually updated for the modern body and the changing needs of the profession.

To achieve the above, this movement training at RADA and Guildhall is founded on swinging exercises, stretching and suppleness, strength, balance, suspension, weight, exploration of imagination and observation. All of these underpin the rest of the training and have a very strong basis in technique. The goal is to achieve this while at the same time developing the ability to become interpreters of the various roles an actor will be called upon to play.

The movement training in the drama school is developmental and accumulative. It consists of several considerations. One part is technical, one part imaginative, and one part is thoughtful. The work is taught in the 'whole part whole' method of teaching. The movement work should not be done in isolation, but alongside all the other subject strands – particularly voice and acting. The actor is encouraged to make links between the different parts of the training, and carry the lessons from one subject strand through to all other areas of their training.

Often a student can have a movement 'break though'[1] during a voice lesson or, conversely, a voice break through in a movement lesson. This is often because the student has warmed up in one lesson and is therefore ready to make progress in the subsequent lesson. It can be something that is affected by a mood, a group-spirited moment, a relaxed moment, or a trusting moment. A break through is directly related to acting better. It is not about being able to achieve a balance in a handstand or achieving a hard dance step or fight move. These are 'closed skills' which, alone, cannot make you a better actor. Nevertheless, achieving a closed skill can go towards an acting break through. Many actors have had such a feeling of euphoria and confidence having mastered an acrobatic trick or dance step that it filters directly into an acting moment.

Considering an example, one student had been trying to achieve a somersault to land on two feet. The week he achieved that he also had to do a long soliloquy in a play and noted that the rush of adrenaline that he experienced during the somersault was the same as the rush of excitement contained in the soliloquy. From the audience's perspective, he was able to deliver the soliloquy with new-found energy. Obviously the best time for a student to have a movement and voice break through is during an acting exercise or performance.

[1] A break through is when a student actor will suddenly be able to achieve something he or she has been working on. It can be something as little as being able to contact the breath, free a stiff shoulder or find the ultimate neutral stance, or as huge as having a moment of being able to move, speak and act all at the same time.

The movement training is collaboration not only of movement styles, but an overlapping of all the training facets – life experience, moods and ideas. It grows like a garden, with care and attention. Starting with getting the earth ready and then planting the seeds, tending them, watering and fertilising them and finally watching them grow strong and tall, with blooms of all different styles. Ending up with a garden bursting with large flowers; small flowers; trees; grasses and bushes. Hopefully by the third year and beyond the actors are as different and as versatile as the best of gardens and continue to develop and blossom into old age, with care and attention.

Movement training is not painting by numbers – that if you do pure movement, Laban, Alexander Technique, period dance, mask work, acrobatics and stage fighting you will automatically become a great actor. These are the tools which help toward the process of great acting, but the individual talent and approach of the student must be knitted with all the other aspects of the training to produce a unique, exciting actor.

It needs the individual talent of the artist to make the craft work. The input of how the student uses the work in collaboration with their talent is what makes it work. It is not tick box learning.

There are students who are brilliant in a single strand, e.g. good movers, who still don't become great actors. There are students who understand intellectually the ideas of the strands, but do not become great actors, and there are students who do not achieve many skills, or struggle with many elements of the training, who go on to be successful actors: this is a mystery to everyone who trains actors.

Bearing in mind the idea of overlapping and developing slowly and surely, the training has been divided up into three main sections. Each section overlaps continuously with the other, but the most relevant exercises, games and movement strands have been placed under the headings:

○ The universal state.
○ Observation.
○ Transformation.

As mentioned earlier, these should not be viewed as three distinct stages; it is not a case of completing one stage before moving onto the next. The overlapping and knitting is inevitable, and imperative, to an integrated training.

Part 1

The universal state

The universal state is commonly known as the neutral state (see Chapter 3, page 23), and is when everybody is in the same physical and mental state for working. It involves getting the actors or students into a state of readiness to be able to work, as individuals and together in a company or chorus.

In this book, the universal state has been divided into two sections: one for the group as a whole and one for the individual actor.

Teaching point

If the individual is to make progress to the universal state, the group must be in the right mind-set to learn. If you are teaching trainee actors, before moving on to any pure movement work I would recommend that you try some of the games and exercises described in Chapter 1. These can help to make the group energised, alert and supportive.

---

1 The universal state for the group

The games

It is very important that actors are dressed neutrally (in black) and learn to let go of any judgement or self-consciousness about body size and shape.

Games are used for fun, fitness, group work, healthy competition, instant imagination and physical bravery with the group. Sessions can start with physical games to warm the body in a fun and imaginative way, getting the blood running through the body and warming up the muscles. Games allow the actors to work quickly, with dexterity and thought, and this in turn takes the emphasis away from body consciousness, and begins the process of releasing any tension.

Although seemingly childish, these games have great value. When they are played with high stakes, they become acting exercises or a series of found moments and physical and emotional relationships. They also work on a secondary level of team building and healthy competition, bringing the feeling of instant joy and playfulness. Games not only warm the actors up physically, but also warm up the level of togetherness or ensemble within the room.

In a drama school setting, the students who enter the room may have come from a range of different lessons – some static, some physical, some emotional, some individual – so the games can unite this group of people, getting them to work together in a fun, simple and very physical way, so they feel relaxed in their bodies and space, and can begin the more challenging physical, imaginative work. Through the simplicity of the games, and the strict rules (where everyone sticks to the same rules every time; the rules of each game are explained in the text) with freedom of spirit, a lot of learning can go into the subconscious, body and mind (i.e. playing as young children do when they learn about many things without intellectualising the process).

Static games, which rely on thought and observation, can be used if the students need to calm down, or regain energy, in the midst of their busy rehearsal schedule.

So, there are games for different purposes and here are a few examples which work well.

Teaching points for games

As soon as you start teaching games, everybody wants to join in which makes it very noisy, confused and ultimately unsafe. Most people will have a previous reference to each game, for example, childhood, but as they are normally handed down, each person, depending on where they come from, will have a different version of it. So when teaching games establish the rules and continue to reinforce them.

Sometimes it may be useful to add an element of 'characterisation' to the game, for example Cat and Mouse can be played as real cats and mice with proper mews and squeaks, and Snakes played as snakes or lizards with hissing and tongues flicking out of the mouths, as practice for, or during an animal study warm up.

All the games could be played 'in character'.

Although the rules in these games are very simple, it is how they are played that is important, and much practice is needed in order to get the most out of them.

Energetic games

Name game 1 – clicking

This game is great for first classes or auditions. It is important for a group to get to know each other, and learning names is a useful place to start. This is true not only for the teacher, but also the students. These games can also introduce the group to use the body to communicate.

1. Stand in a circle and start a rhythm: slap your hands on your knees, then clap your hands together, then click the fingers on your right hand and then on your left. Then say your name.
2. The group repeats your name, e.g. 'knees, hands, click, click, Jackie, JACKIE'.
3. Repeat round the circle until you are back to the beginning.
4. Repeat, getting faster.
5. Send it the other way round.
6. Repeat but say your name with more conviction, at the same time illustrating the intention with a forward, opening and thrusting gesture of the body and arms. The group throws it back.
7. Repeat, but instead of throwing it out there, make any shape with your body that matches your name (don't think about it, do whatever pops out of your body and imagination). The actor's impulse and imagination can be realised.

Variations

When the name game is played in a classroom or at rehearsal, you need to make sure everybody can learn everyone's names. One way to do this is to get one person to run across from one side of the circle to the other and say the name of the person they meet. This second person then runs off to another side of the circle to meet someone else.

You can extend this again by two people running at a time, then three, then four. By this time everybody will be falling about laughing, or it will look like a busy street scene, which could be used in a play.

Teaching point

You will probably find that someone in the class will get stressed and start screeching. This is a good moment to stop and explain that they can run at top speed, and if they relax their arms and shoulders and breathe, they can be strong, quick, direct and without tension, as well as being able to speak without tension.

Name game 2 – marching

1. Form a circle.
2. Set off marching on the spot, knees up to your chin.
3. Count one, two, three, four, and in rhythm, the first person says their name.
4. One, two, three, four, and in rhythm, the person on their left says their name.
5. Repeat for the next person, until everyone in the circle has said their name.
6. Once you've been round the whole circle, repeat the cycle, but march on the count of three and then each person says their name, then two, then one.
7. This is when it can get tense, and when the student can begin on the process described in this book of how to release and free their breath and body.
8. The student runs across the space and says the name of the person opposite, which then sends them off across the circle to the next person.
9. Add two people, then three people, and so forth, adding as many people as you want.

Cat and mouse

This is a chasing game which is good for a new group of people because they can see each other and can be kept calm quite easily, as it is contained in the circle.

The aim of the game is to make the circle as tight as possible and to promote dexterity rather than speed.

First version

1. Take a partner, one person is A, the other B. A is the mouse, B is the cat. Everyone stands in two circles: the As form an inner circle and the Bs form an outer circle. B puts both arms around A.
2. One pair sets off and the cat chases the mouse. If the mouse is tagged, i.e. touched lightly anywhere between the shoulder and the hip, the cat becomes the mouse and the mouse becomes the cat. The new cat chases the new mouse. The mouse tries to find a 'home' which is in front of any other mouse in the circle. The mouse whose home it is needs to very quickly put their arms around the chased mouse so that the chased mouse is safe.
3. When the mouse is safe, the person at the back starts running and is now the mouse, and is chased by the cat, i.e. the cat chases the person behind who becomes the mouse.

4. As the game speeds up the players must be clear in their physicality; there should be no confusion as to who is the cat and who is the mouse.
5. They chase around until the mouse finds a home and that the game continues.

As the players will quickly discover, the circle will become smaller and smaller, because 'home' is in front of A. This is intentional for the game to become strategic, rather than just about who is the fastest player.

The game can be played with energy and speed, or with wits, thought and eye contact. For example, you can run and chase or you can slip over to the couple next to you.

The beauty of this game is that both tactics can be used; both are fine. One person can be charging all over the place when the other one is psychologically dodging.

Variation
Cat and mouse sounds can be made so that the voice is being warmed up as well as the body; the voice can also be used as a way to define who the cat is and who the mouse is.

Second version
○ Partners link arms.
○ One couple starts by the cat chasing the mouse as before. The 'home' for the mouse this time is by linking arms with one end of a pair; the person at the other end must then de-link and become the mouse.

Ships and shores
This is a useful game for warming up bodies physically for more extreme movement and acrobatics. On its own, it works brilliantly to break down barriers of physically contacting one another as well as learning to lift and carry each other. These are abilities actors often need, and this game removes a great deal of anxiety over these issues.

The aim of this game is to win a race. However, it is not just about speed and strength, but also about listening, quick reactions to a situation, feeling, observation and sensitivity to others.

The teacher stands at the front: the wall opposite is 'port', the wall the teacher is standing against is 'starboard', the wall to the right is 'ships', and the wall on their left is 'shores'. The teacher calls out one of these four words, and all the students must run and touch the correct wall as fast as they can. Then you can add the following additional instructions which the students must obey:

1. Climb the rigging. Students mime climbing the rigging or, if there are wall bars or something similar, they can actually climb a 'rigging'.
2. Captain's coming. Students stand fully erect with feet together and salute and say 'Aye, aye, Captain.'
3. Scrub the decks. Students drop quickly to the floor and start to mime scrubbing the decks.
4. Man over board. One student picks up another. The easiest way to pick someone up when you are not warmed up is to do a piggy back, a front piggy back, or a fireman's lift (lifting the person over the shoulder). The hardest way to pick up another person is to pick them up like a baby, regardless of how light the other person is.

5. Crocodiles. Students lie down on their side and clap their arms together like a crocodile snapping its jaws.
6. Freeze. Students absolutely freeze, wherever they are. They are not allowed to move until the teacher says 'unfreeze'. If a student moves before said the teacher has said 'unfreeze', they are out.
7. Unfreeze. This is the command to unfreeze the freeze and the students relax.
8. Submarine. Students lie on their backs with one leg in the air.
9. Bombs overhead. Students curl into a tight little ball like a child's pose or a folded leaf (see page 73).
10. Sharks, 1, 2, 3. Students have to get off the floor by the count of three. They have to find anything in the room to get off the floor; they are not allowed to get back on to the floor until the teacher says 'All clear'. All clear! Is the command to allow everyone to get back onto the floor.

Health and safety
Make sure that you keep an eye on the energy levels of everybody in the group as well as everyone's differing strengths and weaknesses so you can make it as fair as possible. For example, when everybody is running fast to port, say 'Freeze' before they get there, to prevent them from hitting the wall.

The music game
The aim of this game is to bond the group, train quick transformations, and warm up the body and the mind.
Find some really bouncy music (old fashioned rock and roll is always a good choice, as is Stevie Wonder and Carlos Santana).

1. Start with gentle running or skipping.
2. When the students have been going for a few moments stop the music.
3. The students should freeze wherever they are and get into a cat-like position (i.e. ready to pounce), ready for the next instruction.
4. Next, give a command. For example, get into twos, pick somebody up, touch something green, kiss someone on the neck, butterfly kiss someone, hug someone tightly, hug someone softly (all these are a fun way to get used to these particular problems which can often arise in acting situations).
5. The last person to do this will be out.

Teaching points
So that the students don't hurt themselves physically (or psychologically, in the case of kissing and hugging), make some hard rules at the beginning of the game.
Only one person can pick another person up, not several people picking up one person.
As the teacher, you need to keep an eye on their energy because this game can be physically exhausting, and the aim is to get the body and mind warmed up, but not exhausted. In the class there will be students of varying levels of fitness.

Often you will find that the person who wins is not always the quickest or the strongest. There are many ways to win using abilities other than speed: the powers of observation, dexterity, relaxation and psychology can be used.

Musical chairs

The purpose of this game is to become quick but polite; this game could be used in a period drama.

1. Place enough chairs in a line, one for each member of the class, minus one, with the seats facing alternately inwards and outwards.
2. The teacher plays the music and the class walks round in a clockwise direction.
3. When the music stops everybody sits on a chair.
4. The person without a chair is out.

Variation

You could play this with different steps, for example, skipping, hopping or jumping, or you could play it as an animal.

Jailors

The purpose of this exercise is to warm up the body and mind, and can also be used to warm up a cast for period drama.

1. Put enough chairs out for half the class to sit on, plus two spare chairs.
2. There should be one person sitting on every chair except one, and one person standing behind every chair, including the empty one.
3. The people behind the chairs are jailors and the people sitting are the prisoners.
4. The aim is for the jailor behind the empty chair to get it filled with a prisoner. To do this the jailor behind the empty chair must wink at a prisoner. If the prisoner sees him wink, then he has to run across to the chair and sit on it, without being tagged by their own jailor.
5. If the prisoner is tagged before they reach the empty chair, then they sit back down in their old seat.
6. If the prisoner manages to escape, then the jailor with the newly empty chair will need to wink at the prisoners and try to fill their chair.
7. The game continues like this until the teacher ends it.

Snakes

The aim of the game is to warm up the body and mind, particularly for warming up for the reptiles in an animal study.

1. One person lies on the ground and is the snake.
2. The rest of the group puts a finger on the snake.

3. When the snake decides, they lash out with their arms and legs and try to catch as many people as they can in one go. They can only wriggle on their stomach (using arms and legs).
4. Once the snake has caught someone, then they too become a snake and have to wriggle along on their stomach. The aim is for the snakes is to catch as many people as they can.
5. The others try to leap out of the way of the snakes.
6. The last person to be caught becomes the new snake for the next round.

Stuck in the mud

This is a quick and easy way to warm everybody up in a fun and physical way.

1. One person is the chaser.
2. They run after everybody else, trying to catch as many people as they can.
3. The chaser tags them somewhere between the shoulders and hips. If they manage to tag someone, then that person has to stand still with their legs and arms wide apart. A free person crawls between the legs of the person who has been 'stuck', in order to free them. Whilst they are between the legs they are safe from being tagged, but as soon as they come out from between the legs then they are vulnerable to being caught again.
4. If the chaser gets everybody, then another person becomes the chaser.

If the class is older or dressed inappropriately for crawling between each other's legs, then the stuck people can be freed by free people running under their arms.

Sticky sticky glue

The aim of this game is to listen for clues in the person's breath and watching their body language. After the initial story, it is about running and dodging. This can be played like Snakes, on the stomach, or on the feet.

1. One person is 'it' with their hands splayed out in front of them. Everyone elses hold a finger.
2. The person who is 'it' makes up a story. When they say the word 'glue' everyone is released. If they get tagged by the 'it' person, they have to sit out.
3. If it is played like snakes, it is the snake who makes up the story.

Here's an example of a story:

> 'I was walking along the road and I saw some sticky, sticky . . .TREES!
> I then carried on and looked in the shop window and saw some sticky, sticky . . . BUNS!
> Then I carried on walking down the road along an alley, up a mountain and found some sticky, sticky . . . GLUE!!!!'

Pirates

1. Put floor mats out all over the space, with enough gaps to jump from mat to mat.
2. One person is the pirate and the rest of the class are the shipmates.

3. The pirate counts to ten and the shipmates run away.
4. The pirate then has to run after the shipmates and catch as many as they can, without anyone (even the pirate) touching the floor.
5. If the shipmates touch the floor then they are out and have to sit out.
6. If the pirate touches the floor then everybody is back in again.
7. If the pirate catches the shipmates then they sit out and if the pirate catches everybody then the last person is then the pirate.

Sense games

The sense games are useful for the student to become aware of people other than themselves, and to use their senses of hearing, smell and touch to explore communication, trust and space.

Blind tag

This game is a good lead up to blind lead (see p. 113), or a class that is using the senses.

1. Everybody shuts their eyes and spaces themselves out around the room.
2. One person is the chaser.
3. The chaser is given a bunch of keys, and as they move they shake the keys until they manage to catch another member of the group who then receives the keys and becomes the chaser. The teacher makes sure no one comes to any harm.
4. The chaser can only stop shaking the keys if they stop moving and wait and listen to try to hear where their classmates are so they can catch them.
5. As soon as they start again they must shake the keys.

Grandmother's footsteps

The aim of this exercise is for the body to be extremely quiet and still. It encourages suspension, stillness and focus.

1. One person, the grandmother, stands at the top of the room and the rest of the group stand at the other end of the room.
2. The grandmother turns her back on the group and everybody else creeps up towards her from behind.
3. When the grandmother turns around, everybody else has to be completely still.
4. If the grandmother sees anybody move then they have to return to their starting place.
5. The person who gets to the grandmother before she sees them move, becomes the new grandmother.

Variations

This game can be played during an animal study class. For example, primates, elephants, cats, birds, etc, using animal sounds to distract the grandmother from seeing who is moving. This way the animals are being practised and the students can discover the challenges of the animals' physicality and rhythm.

To make it more of a company exercise you can play it with a bunch of keys, being the grandmother's treasure.

The aim of this variation is for the group or company to get the keys back to their den, so the group finds a way of working as a team.

○ A bunch of keys is placed at the grandmother's feet and the rest of the group creeps up and, just as before, anyone who is moving when the grandmother turns around has to return to the starting point.
○ When someone gets to the grandmother, the keys must be stolen and returned to the starting point without the her seeing them.

This can be done in anyway the group decides, but the rules are:

○ If the grandmother sees someone with the keys, the keys go back to the grandmother and the person who was holding the keys goes back home.
○ If the person who has the keys moves then they go back home and the keys return to the grandmother.
○ The group wins when they get the keys back to the beginning.
○ The grandmother wins if she manages to stop them within a time limit.
○ If the grandmother sees the person with the keys, even if they were not moving, they have to put the keys back and go back to the beginning.
○ It does not count if the grandmother hears the keys: the group can rattle the keys and distract the grandmother as much as they want, so that while she watches for one person moving others sneak up and tags her. This reiterates the aim of the game, which is for the group to work together. The **group** has won when the keys are back at the beginning.

N.B. Make sure the grandmother is very strict in these games.

Who stole the honey from the honey pot?

The aim of this game is to use the sense of hearing and the quality of creeping and suspension.

1. The class sits in a circle and one person (the bear) sits in the middle with the keys (the honey) on the floor behind them.
2. One person gets up and very quietly and stealthily creeps over and take the keys, creeping back to their place and sitting down again.
3. Then the entire group places their hands behind their backs and says:
   'Wake up Mr Bear. Who stole the honey from the honey pot?'
4. The bear wakes up and, using their observational skills, looks at the faces in the class, trying to find who is guilty.
5. The bear tries to guess who it is; they have three chances. If they get it right they change places with the person who took the keys.

Mime telephones

The aim of this exercise is for the mime to be absolutely precise to the story, so that the non-verbal physicalisation is clear to the observer.

1. Form two groups; A and B.
2. Group B waits outside the room. Group A devises a story for one person to mime. There must not be any other characters in the scene. An example of a story would be: You are a robber. You search a road in the dark for the house you are going to rob. You climb up a drain pipe, and fall to the ground. You try to pick the lock on the door, but it won't open. You try to open the window, it slides up so you climb in. You manage to get some different objects in your swag bag. Just as you are climbing the stairs, you hear a noise. You panic. You drop your swag and start running. You are shot in the back and fall.
3. The first person from group B comes in, and someone from group A mimes the story.
4. A second person from group B then enters the room. The first person from group B repeats the mime in front of the second person from group B. A third person from group B enters, and the second group B person repeats the mime to them, and so one until each person in group B has performed the mime and passed on the story.
5. Each person mimes exactly what they saw, so if the mime had moments of distraction or giggling in, then these should remain in the mime. The game is like Chinese whispers; the mime will change slightly with each new student.
6. At the end, and starting backwards, each person describes what they have just done and what they think they were doing.
7. Sometimes the result is that everybody does the same and guesses correctly, and sometimes it just gets more and more inaccurate.

Static games

The purpose of these games is to bring a class into the universal state, when they are exhausted from previous rehearsals or classes (or full of food after lunch). The games use observation and perception, which are skills that are often needed in acting.

Essence

This is a good, calming game which allows members of the group to observe each other's personalities, using elements, materials, animals and matters as describing aids.

1. Sit in a circle.
2. One person is in the 'hot seat' and thinks of another person in the group.
3. Go around the group, asking 'If this person were a ... what sort of ... would they be'. It has to be a question which leads to the 'essence' of the character, and not factual information or physical descriptions. For example, 'If this person were a fruit, animal, breakfast cereal, type of light, genre of film, music, dance etc.' The question cannot contain any type of human element, even things such as 'If this person were a

Simpson, which Simpson would they be?' They could ask, for example 'If this person were an American cartoon, which cartoon would they be?'

4. When everybody has had a question answered in the circle, go around the group again with everyone repeating the answer they had to their question. In this way, a full picture of the person should emerge.
5. Then go around the circle, and ask each person who they think it is.
6. When everybody has guessed, the person in the 'hot seat' will reveal their answer.

Mafia

This is a good team building exercise, as it involves working together, reading body language and acting. It works in rounds, each round including a Mafia killing and the town's people guessing.

1. The group sits in a circle and are the townspeople.
2. The teacher is on the outside of the circle and is God. God knows everything that is going on, will not change the rules or give anything away to anyone. He is neutral.
3. The townspeople shut their eyes and God goes around the circle and taps two people on the head who will become the Mafia. Note: the Mafia's job is to kill off all the townspeople in rounds.
4. God then goes around the circle and chooses one bodyguard. Note: the bodyguard's job is to save someone at every round, i.e. when God asks the bodyguard to wake up then he points to one person to save from a Mafia killing (he is allowed to save himself once in a game).
5. God chooses one person to be a policeman. Note: the policeman's job is to learn something about one person every round. For example, when God asks him to open his eyes, and everybody else's are shut, he points to one of the circle and God will indicate to him if they are a townsperson, Mafia or a bodyguard.
6. God taps the policeman on the head, who wakes up and indicates to God which of the townspeople he would like to know about.
7. Then God draws in the air an M for Mafia, a B for bodyguard and a T for townsperson and then the policeman shuts his eyes.
8. God taps the body guard on the head, who opens his eyes and indicates which of the town's people he would like to save.
9. Everybody opens their eyes and God says who has been killed. That person leaves the circle and is not allowed to say anything to the group.
10. Conversation round. The townspeople now discuss who they think the Mafia are and the Mafia disguise themselves as townspeople. There are absolutely no rules about whether anybody in the group can lie and pretend they are the policeman, the bodyguard, a townsperson or Mafia, so the others have to be on the lookout for bad acting or body language or someone even telling the truth. The more often you play, the more people can read the way you play, so the challenge then becomes having to find different ways of playing it.

    When the discussions have gone on for a while, try to encourage people to listen to each other and not just come out with their own opinions.
11. God goes round the circle and asks each person to name someone they think is the Mafia. When a person says a name, the person must hold up one finger.

12. The person with the most fingers up at the end is out and they are allowed to say one thing to the rest of the group which may be of help or maybe a lie.
13. Then the game begins all over again with the group not knowing, except perhaps the policeman whether or not there are two Mafia left or only one.
14. The game is over either when there are no Mafia left, then the townspeople have won, or when there are no townspeople left, then he Mafia have won.

Rules

Set the rules up clearly at the beginning of the game.

○ The bodyguard can only save themselves once.
○ God cannot change the rules during the game.
○ God cannot give help to anybody.
○ The dead townspeople (or angels) are not allowed to make any noise or comments about what is going on in the game after they are dead.

2 Space, dimension and rhythm

Space and sensitivity

Spatial awareness is crucial for the actor for many reasons. Firstly, many of our relationships with others depend on the space between us. Secondly, very often a play will move from a small theatre to a large one, and an actor must be able to fill the different spaces with their body and voice and maintain the ease with which they do this. Finally, it is important for the actor to be able to communicate in the largest of spaces and in spaces as small as a those created by a TV or film camera. Most classes will begin with a space exercise of some sort or another. What is difficult for the teacher to achieve is to make sure that the student actors remain aware of the importance of space when they move to another class or appear on stage.

> **Teaching point**
> *After doing an exercise, it is important to discuss the reasons for the exercise and the lessons learnt, so that students can make links between the movement work and their other classes.*

The ball game

This is not so much a game but rather training in the use of space, chorus work and a state of readiness as a whole. It is tough at first, because there will be people in your class who are brilliant at ball games (in a competitive fashion) and who instantly become competitive and there will be people who absolutely hate them and instantly become defensive and stiff. Try to get everyone to realise that the point of the exercise is communication and working together to support the weakest in the group, and not about catching and throwing.

Aims and observations of the game

The shoulders should end up being open; the hand extended but soft, and the legs strong and wide; the feet like cats' paws (ready to pounce). The ball should not be heard. When the exercise is really flowing, take away one person to watch. Send them back in and choose someone else to watch until the whole class has observed the exercise. This gives everyone a rest and allows them to appreciate each other. When it's perfect with the ball, take the ball away. Keep the same rules, keep it flowing. Notice how hard it is to remember the space once you have taken away the ball.

Choose a ball which is smaller and softer than a football, but not too small. It should be neutral in colour as playing with a football it is too tempting to turn it into a game of football. This exercise is about giving and receiving energy, and communication.

Nobody is allowed to apologise and nobody is allowed to blame anybody else.

Make sure you give all this exercise plenty of time so that everybody gets used to the new way of working.

1. Form a circle with the teacher standing in the middle with the ball.
2. To begin with the teacher throws the ball to everyone in the circle in turn. The ball is then thrown back to the teacher; this way everyone gets a feel for the weight of the ball and the energy to throw it back and forth.
3. Put the ball down and get everyone to stand in a natural, neutral stance.
4. Take a deep breath in and everybody lifts their bodies and arms up, and falls back onto the right leg with the right arm falling back into the lunge.
5. Push back up off that leg and bring everything back up again to neutral.
6. Keep repeating on the right and left, right and left. There should be a feeling of release, freedom and suspension through your own space.
7. Throw the ball through the air, with no spin and ensuring that you send it with enough energy to reach the recipient with ease. The teacher sends it back and forth to each student in the circle. The person who receives it reaches up with both arms and then steps back on the right leg as the ball goes from a fully stretched arm and finger tips and softens into the right hand. There has to be total softness otherwise if the hand is stiff and tense, the ball will bounce off.
8. This person then throws it in a big arc back to the teacher, who breathes in and falls back onto the right leg.
9. Go all the way round the circle and back again.
10. Draw the group's attention to the good examples and be patient with the people who find it hard. There should be control, freedom and elasticity, suspension and release, and strength.
11. When the group has mastered this on both right and left sides, add additional rules:
    ○ Shutting your eyes on receiving the ball, and throw it back with eyes shut. This adds trust and sensitivity to the situation.
    ○ Without the ball, the students run around the room, ensuring that there is equal space between them; this achieves the effect of 'balancing the space'.
    ○ Add the ball. Throw it and everybody runs whilst the ball is in the air. The person who is in the space where the ball falls then catches it, bending deep into their legs.
    ○ Everybody else does the same, ball-less.
    ○ Everybody holds in a suspended state until the ball is sent through the air again and then everybody runs into the empty space.

○ Do the exercise with your eyes shut on catching the ball, and sending the ball. Don't forget that as soon as you send the ball, you run also. There should be a sense of ease, space, freedom, suspension and release.

Friend and enemy

1. Walk around the room, looking at all the danger points for stubbing your toes or knocking into something. Look at each other in a way that is as 'normal' as possible so that everybody looks natural.
2. Start running gently. Then in your mind's eye find somebody in the group who is your friend and somebody else who is your enemy. Put your friend between you and your enemy and keep them there. Keep running as best as you can.
3. Stop!
4. Repeat this exercise several times.

Lines and curves

1. Work in pairs. One person is A and the other is B.
2. A sets off in an easy floor pattern, just walking at first, and then stops. A changes direction and as A sets of into another easy floor pattern, B walks A's original floor pattern, keeping an eye on A's second pattern. Keep this going (and keep it easy to start with).
3. Change over so that B is now leading and A follows B.
4. Change partners if you wish and then add different floor patterns, for example, zig-zags or curls. The leader, however, needs to keep their eye on the person following them and if they find they are not keeping up then the leader should try using simpler patterns.
5. Now start adding different ways of moving and make sure the person who is following you is doing it right, both keeping up with the special floor patterns and also keeping up with the rhythms and steps.
6. Now put everybody in groups of three and do this again and then groups of four or five.
7. The more people who are doing it the harder it is, but it can be very interesting.
8. Each couple, threesome and foursome can then make different sounds. This takes a lot of listening to be able to really hear your own people. It is possible but needs the utmost of concentration.

◉ Feeling for each other (DVD: Exercise 1)

This movement exercise works wonders for companies at the start of rehearsals, as well as in later stages of production, when relationships are getting stale or the company is moving venue and you need to explore space again. It is very good for sensitivity and space.

1. Walk around the space, as naturally as possible. This can be quite hard to do as you feel quite unnatural.
2. Explore the space and make sure that you see the whole room as well as the other people in the group. Also, try to see the people for the first time but try not to act this. (This is always quite hard, especially when the group knows each other well.)
3. When the whole group has calmed down, and don't start this if there is a any kind of giggling or unsettled energy, reach out and touch somebody else's finger tips and at the same time look that person in the eyes.

4. Keep moving and then touch someone else's finger tips, but do not let go of the other person while you are finding the new person. You are also not allowed to be all alone in the space, or grab at anyone.

5. Next do the same with the elbows, then neck, hips, and forehead, always trying to maintain contact with the eyes, not looking at the parts of the body in question. It is much easier where there are two sides to your body e.g. arms or legs rather than head, but it is worth a try.

6. Then go back to the finger tips, which will give you a great release in your arms and neck, and then try to walk around the space still reaching but don't touch now. Just imagine you are touching. Still reach and look into each other's eyes. This will help the student to realise the sensation of contact between people. The touching will then keep the physical sensation of touching when no actual contact takes place.

7. Put more and more space between you and the person you are looking at, but you will find that the whole room is connected in the most wonderful way.

8. Then bring it back, closer and closer until you are touching again, and you will be filled with the most marvellous feeling of togetherness.

Shoal of fish

In a shoal of fish, all the fish move as a group; you cannot tell who is leading, and messages seem to spread silently and instantaneously through the shoal. This is what actors hope to achieve when working as an ensemble or chorus.

1. Start with the whole group running together.
2. Try not to have a leader.
3. Keep the group moving like a shoal of fish.
4. Start marching.
5. The teacher taps one person on the shoulder and they have to change the rhythm. This person doesn't have to be at the front, so the rest of the group has to be able to feel it. This will happen like a ripple effect from the person next to the rhythm changer and so on through the group.
6. When the group has firmly got the idea about the rhythms being in their bodies, then move on to adding sound.

Observations

Notice how easily the movement is neglected as soon as you add the voice. Incorporating movement and voice is an on-going problem for the actor. Keep changing the leader until everybody has had a go.

Circle rhythms

Circle rhythms are helpful because the class is still working as a group, but now everyone is able to be creative in an individual way. As the rhythm is passed around the circle, each member of the group is inspired by the previous member, but is also allowed to change the rhythm and make it their own.

1. Sit in a circle.
2. One person taps a rhythm on the floor using their body and hands and adds a vocal sound.

3. Keeping it quite simple, they repeat it until it becomes natural.
4. They then turn to the person on their right and give them the rhythm.
5. This person in turn starts tapping that same rhythm. When they have it they keep it going for about four times.
6. They then transform it into a rhythm of their own.
7. They in turn make sure that it becomes theirs and then they pass it on to the next person.
8. This gets passed on around the circle until everyone has led the rhythm. At this stage the whole group moves together.
9. They in their turn keep it going and eventually the whole group is moving in rhythm together.

⊙ High, low, wide, narrow (DVD: Exercises 2 & 3)

The rules of the diagonals, and high, low, wide, narrow, are strict. In the rules, the actor finds freedom. The imagination and exploration is confined in the strict form. The idea is simple, but the possibilities are boundless. It contains the actor in the physical space, and although this can be difficult for some actors, as they feel it is prohibiting the freedom of expression, it is good training for the blocking of a play, where the actor has a particular place to be, but needs to fill it with imagination and transformation.

The following numbered points are the instructions given to the class by the teacher. What the class do with it will be as individual as each student present. Once the students have the rules firmly ingrained in their body, they can use it for specific play and character needs.

1. Stand in a space.
2. When the teacher bangs the drum, the student stretches their body as high as it will go.
3. When the drum is banged again, go as low as you can in your own body (make sure you do not lie flat because this would, of course, be wide and low, not just low).

On each bang of the drum:

4. Make your body as wide as it can be.
5. Make it as narrow as it can be.
6. Make your body go as far forward as it can in the space, without moving off the spot.
7. Make your body go as far back as it can without moving it off the spot. Your face must remain turned to the front wall, even if your body is turned towards the back wall. If you turn your body and you face towards the back wall, this means the back wall becomes the new front wall.
8. Make sure thought and imagination go with these movements, for example, when the body goes narrow, have narrow-minded thoughts and intentions.
9. The teacher keeps banging the drum, and as soon as they say one of the commands, you need to go straight into it.

Variation 1

Firstly change the dynamics: fast, slow, medium, so, you could say slow high; fast low; slow wide; slow narrow; fast forward; and slow backward.

Variation 2

○ Get into pairs, one person is A, the other B.
○ A leads. If A goes fast high, then B does this straight afterwards. If A goes wide fast, then B does it straight afterwards.
○ Change over so B leads.
○ Split the class into two groups, A and B, so each side can see each other. (It can look very dramatic.)
○ If A goes slow low, B will answer with fast high. If A does slow wide, B will answer with fast narrow. If A does slow back then B will do fast forward.
○ Split the class into two further groups so they can watch each other.

Variation 3

○ Divide the students into groups of four.
○ Have three on one side and one on the other, facing each other.
○ When the single student stretches slowly up, then the other three stretch slowly up.
○ When the single student goes fast wide, then the other three go fast wide.
○ Keep repeating.
○ Change the leader, and this time if the leader does slow narrow, the other three answers with fast wide.
○ Keep repeating.

Variation 4

○ Divide the class into two large groups facing each other across the space.
○ One group leads and they repeat the exercise above, so if one group goes high slow, the other group goes high slow.
○ Then change it so if one group does forward quick, then the other group does backward slow, and so on.

Variation 5

○ Divide the class into two separate groups.
○ Let the group explore the concept of their whole group going high low, wide narrow forward and back. Not just inside the actor himself, but as the whole group. You then get a very dramatic image of, say, high going very high with one of the group being lifted to the highest point, or even climbing up on pillars and posts.
○ Let the groups watch each other again.
○ You then can let the groups relate to each other and repeat the exercises above.

Variation 6

○ When you have worked on the elements, you could also incorporate this into the exercise. For example one group could do high, low, wide, narrow, forward, back and do it as fire.
○ Another group could do it as water.
○ You could see what happens when the fire meets the water or the earth meets the air.

☉ Diagonals (DVD: Exercise 4)

This term is a little misleading as it is a term for an exercise which is not only the diagonals but a horizontal as well. This exercise encourages the actor to fill the space on offer, and may be helpful for preparing actors to work in theatre, where they have to communicate across an auditorium through 'diagonal lines', up to the people in the Gods, and down to the people at the back of the stalls.

This exercise can be quite difficult for some people to master, and like anything, some people find tough rules hard to stick to.

1. Start by walking the entire length of the room along one wall.
2. Then walk down the breadth, then the length of the room and finally the breadth again. This enables the shapes to be absorbed into the memory.
3. Then start at the bottom left back corner, squat ,and draw your finger along the bottom length of the wall.
4. Do the same along the bottom breadth of the wall, then the other bottom breadth and length.
5. Do the same reaching up on tip toes to the highest point of the lengths and breadths.
6. Go to the top left corner and draw the vertical line to the bottom left corner.
7. Go to the top right and draw the line down from the top to the bottom, then do the same in the other two corners.
8. Then start at the back top corner and draw a line through the space from the left top corner, through the diagonal to the bottom right corner.
9. Then go to the bottom left corner and draw a line through the diagonal to the top right corner.
10. Then start from the top left corner and draw a line through the space to the bottom right corner and then draw a line along the front horizontal to the left bottom corner.
11. Your only choice from there is to draw a diagonal line through the space from the bottom left hand corner to the top right hand corner.
12. You can then choose to either go along the back horizontal from the right corner to the left corner *or* you can choose to go along the right hand horizontal.
13. You can never go down the vertical.
14. Come into the centre of the room and face the front.

As with high, low, wide, narrow, you are not allowed to face anywhere but the front. The student can stand on a square mat and draw imaginary walls up from the floor square of the mat. This helps people who find spatial work difficult.

Let the students explore the horizontal and diagonals in their own cube only using their body.

Variation 1

Run or walk, skip or hop the diagonals and use the entire space. Bring it down to just the size of your body. Bring it further down to just a mere breath and communicate the diagonals head, breath and face.

☉ Variation 2 (DVD: Exercise 5)

o Get into pairs, standing next to each other.

○ Start at different points in the space, either top corner or bottom corner.

○ Start exploring crossing the diagonals with each other and see what dramatic ideas they may evoke. The students could be witches casting a spell. They could be painting a house.

○ Do exactly the same diagonals and horizontals and work together.

○ Add another group and another until you are filling the whole of the space. This could be a busy street scene or a half price sale, all reaching for something new to try on. The students could be fire, wind, earth, or air.

○ Choose a story or a scenario that the students can communicate through these diagonal movements and show the rest of the group.

Movement in practice

When working on a Greek tragedy this is a very good pure movement exercise to help the chorus work together as one entity. Along with the purity of the high, low, wide, narrow and the exercises above, with the protagonist starting and the chorus responding, it is possible for extremes of emotion to be used.

1. Warm the cast up by chewing (stretching the facial, tongue and neck muscles), rib stretches (see p. 47), accentuating the use of the dimensions high, and wide, forward during the rib stretches.

2. Using the bouncing and shaking down through the spine exercise (see p. 50), swing the arms and full torso swings, using the dimensions high, low, suspension and release.

3. Guide the group through individual, high, low, wide, narrow, forward and back, making sure that they are beginning to think of the play in hand.

4. Ask the whole group to do it, getting them high, low, wide, and narrow, forward and back.

5. Ask the one person to be the protagonist (with students, as part of their training, this can be done experimentally before it has been cast, so everybody can have a go as the protagonist. Obviously if it is a professional play and time is of the essence and all the actors have their roles, use the real protagonist and the real chorus).

6. Everybody spreads out around the room. If the protagonist goes high, everybody will sympathise and go high also.

7. Secondly if he goes low everybody will go high.

8. If he goes slow high, everybody else goes slow high in sympathy.

9. If he goes slow high, everybody else goes fast high.

10. If he goes slow high, everybody else goes fast low.

11. Do the same but add extreme emotion as well. For example, if he laughs, everybody else laughs too, or if he cries they do the opposite and laugh.

12. Keep exploring all possibilities, encouraging the chorus to move as one, filling their movement with emotion and intention, in response to the protagonist.

The above exercises were used by Jackie to inform her movement directing during rehearsals for the Greek tragedy *The Burial at Thebes* by Lucy Pitman-Wallace.

3 The universal state for the individual

The universal state for the individual is when the actor's body is in a neutral state ready to speak and act freely, and to transform.

Stance and posture

Obviously not every part an actor plays requires them to have a good posture; many characters actually have a bad posture. However, a good posture is needed because the actor needs a neutral place from which to transform, so that the voice does not get locked in by tension in the neck and shoulders, for example.

One of the hardest things for an actor to do is to find a natural stance which enables them to be free and open with no habits cluttering up the natural self, and allowing the breath and voice to be accessed without tension, and the physical imagination to be open and free and without inhibition. The physical imagination is the body's response to what is in the head. The physical imagination cannot be released if the body is blocked in any way, as we will describe later. In this neutral state, an actor should be able to be entirely still, but remain a listening, receptive body that is filled with energy. Obviously, the longer the actor has been training in movement work, the easier it is for them to achieve this.

To achieve this, stand with the feet flat on the floor, shoulder width apart, with the knees released, and the torso erect and vertical, but not tense. This results in a stable stance with the centre of gravity at about the level of the pelvis. Keeping the centre of gravity low allows the back and abdominal muscles to be used more effectively in breath support. (If you stand with your feet together and your knees locked, your centre of gravity moves upwards and the back and abdominal muscles have to become more actively engaged to maintain balance to remain standing.)

The ability to control breathing while speaking or acting can be adversely affected in various ways. Dizziness caused by medications, alcohol, drugs, neuropathies, inner ear disease, and visual dysfunction result in excessive engagement of the back and abdominal muscles to help maintain balance, thus lessening the use of these muscles for breath support. Anxiety, grief, and other emotions involve tension of many of the muscles in the back and abdomen and alter the breathing pattern. Any of these can affect the ability to control and provide sufficient breath support when speaking and acting.

The posture needs a free neck; lengthened and broad spine and back; free pelvis and knees. This posture comes from the time in our lives when we can stand and walk but before we have built up bad habits. These habits may be due to natural development at puberty, in particular speedy growth, or they may come about as a result of specific physical training for activities such as dance or sport. They may simply result from subconscious copying of parents and siblings or injuries incurred over time. Some of these things will affect the students when they come to be trained.

Neutrality

Neutrality is a crucial principal in actor training. It is a state where the actor attains energised stillness. It is 'a state of readiness' (Copeau), from which any movement or action can begin. The neutral state is not a passive state, but a potent one. It is a place of calm and a place full of vitality. It allows the body to be fully receptive.

In the first lesson, it is helpful to use imagery to support this feeling and physicality; then as the students have more classes and the work develops, the more it becomes a natural physical feat.

In Russian director, Vsevolod Meyerhold's biomechanics, the neutral position is quite specific:

- Feet are parallel.
- Hands are by the hips.
- Fingers point towards the floor.
- Eyes look towards a point in the distance.
- The weight is slightly forward and the knees are released (or very slightly bent).

Achieving neutral

Achieving a neutral state does not mean getting rid of the actor's personality or natural talent. However, if they can reach moments of neutrality and the pursuit of neutrality purifies them, it can make their very errors more commanding.

Beneath every character the actor becomes is a near neutral state. Movement training helps to identify a resting state for the actor, a condition of presence from which all things evolve, and to which all action reverts.

The movement teacher might start with imaginative exercises such as the following:

'Imagine you are standing on a hill top. You are a tree. Your legs, torso and head are the trunk, your arms are the branches and your finger tips are the leaves.

Imagine your feet are connected to the grass with the roots of the tree growing down deep into the earth. Your body, because it is a growing tree, is not stiff, but filled with the energy of a living organism.

Open your arms out into the sky like branches in the air. A slight wind blows through you and your leaves gently rustle in the wind. The human in you looks down over the hills. Thus the movement becomes filled and thoughtful.'

The student should understand that the aim of neutrality is not only to release the breath and allow full vocal support, but also to provide a good starting point for all imaginative transformations.

The importance of pure movement for the voice

'It is said that the body speaks before the voice and of course that must be true. When we have an impulse to communicate with words or sound, muscles work to allow the lungs to expand and take in air, that air is propelled across the vocal folds to produce sound, the sound is enhanced by resonance and shaped into words. Words or language are a physical gesture of thought, intention and feeling, a physical gesture of expression as silent movement may be. A thought begins to be expressed with movement deep inside the core of the body, opening and widening the internal space for air and in a sense also opening for the thought to take shape; the whole body then supports the movement of air which carries that thought, the body and the voice are one. Movement can exist without sound, but sound doesn't exist without movement. Voice teachers are indebted to the great movement teachers.'

ELLEN NEWMAN, VOICE SPECIALIST AND FORMER HEAD OF VOICE, RADA

It is important to remember that the lungs are three dimensional. The expansion of the lungs should be down in the abdomen and out on all sides. Inhalations should involve relaxation of the abdomen and back muscles, and exhalation should involve a sustained and controlled contraction of the abdominal and, to a lesser extent, the back muscles. Proper posture therefore needs to be maintained to allow this to happen.

Obviously, when you are 'in character', you will need to be able to speak well, but we also need to take into consideration that when you are is acting, you are not always standing in a correct posture and breathing 'correctly'. After all, most parts are emulating real people, and not everybody stands upright, breathing in a controlled way. So it is really important to start movement training by establishing a good posture and good breathing which can then be adapted to change bodily behaviour to suit a particular character without interfering too much with breath support.

In the early stages of their training, acting students are so busy trying to achieve a proper posture that it is often hard for them to achieve physical transformation at the same time as maintaining good breath support. By the end of the second year of training, they usually have a good enough posture and creative imagination to be able to combine the two.

Through movement training, a good free strong natural posture will eventually be achieved by activities involving stretching, swinging and releasing, arching and rounding the spine thus building strength and suppleness in the legs and torso. The ability to achieve this elementary good posture is a long process.

Tension and release

Tension can be when the muscles are fully engaged and locked. It can also be a psychological state, which stops the body being able to move freely. Release is when one lets go of the tension.

Actors need to achieve physical and psychological tension and release, depending on the different characters they are playing. It is important for the actor to use the tension or release, which is needed for the character, and to be able to discard tension or release that is not relevant to the character, or that is personal to the actor.

Releasing tension allows the body to be in a state of readiness to be able to explore the breath and the physical expression of the imagination or, as it can be called, 'physical imagination'. This is where the body expresses fully what is in the imagination. That is, the actor fully manifests what is in their head, through to their body and physicality. This cannot work if the actor is full of unwanted tension or old habitual tensions.

Releasing tension does not mean the body is saggy and floppy with no energy or muscle support. On the contrary, the body needs to have plenty of muscle and strength to support it, but not so much that it gets in the way. For example, if the torso is too built up with shaped muscle it becomes impossible for the actor to transform physically. Also it tightens the voice and the voice can become restricted. The body needs muscularity but not useless, empty muscles. There are some actors who have built up their muscles but find it hard to lift another person, and injure themselves very easily. On the other hand, there are others who are small but strong and flexible who can easily lift people twice their size.

The point is that if you want to be an actor who can transform then you must keep your body healthy and strong and your own habits obscured. Once all your habits have been discarded, they can always be called back for character choice but at least they will be a choice and not an inconvenience which blocks choice.

Each day some part of the body may need more attention than others, and for this there are specific exercises to release and free and strengthen each part of the body. Each exercise can be done alone or with others as a whole class exercise.

'Release' is a word that is often used in relation to the breath, knees or spine. It feels very much like relaxation, but with some tension to keep you on your feet.

When you are balancing, after engaging all your muscles to achieve the shape of your balance, be it standing on both feet, a headstand, handstand, a balance on one leg or a balance on risen toes, then you just breathe out and let the muscles go a little, which then allows the body to soften slightly and the balance to take place more effectively than through using body tension.

On two feet, you can do the same thing, i.e. squeeze all the muscles in the body, including the face, and then let everything go. At that point the body is free and without muscular tension, it allows for the jaw to drop and the breath to travel freely through.

4 Pure movement to achieve neutral

The following isolation exercises encourage an articulate body.

The pure movement, in particular the release-based swings and The Cat, train the actor in body tension and body release. The pure movement training, with The Cat, is the fundamental, physical training for the actor. With use of imagination and physical technique, the actor gains an articulate body which can then easily transform and respond to the psychological aspect of a character.

Pure movement is the conjunction of many body exercises which have their basis in release, weight, suspension and space. The aim of pure movement is primarily functional, to get the body in a ready state for voice and acting. It is the basis from which all other work springs. Every movement, voice and acting lesson can benefit from starting with pure movement. Animal study, period dance, acrobatics, Laban, mask work and stage fighting all work better when they begin with pure movement and when the pure movement is infiltrated throughout the class.

'Pure acrobatic movement helps students be brave and dexterous in falling, leaping, jumping, turning, balancing and lifting.

The continuous repetition and development of the release, strength, suppleness, fitness and imagination of the pure movement gives them the ability and inclination for transformation and to feel they can do anything that is demanded of them. Compared to those who haven't been trained an actor with a training in and understanding of pure movement is more adaptable in performance.

Whilst there is crossover in some elements of the pure movement and stage combat, the core elements of strength, fitness, balance and suppleness serve as a strong base for stage combat work to build upon.'

RICHARD RYAN, FIGHT DIRECTOR

It is vital for the imagination to be engaged when doing pure movement, because it is essential that the pure movement is not only warming up the body, but also the mind and the imagination.

> **Teaching point**
>
> *It is important for the teacher to use their voice to feed the student's imagination. Try to use imaginative images to avoid the movement being robotic and empty.*
>
> *When the student engages the imagination into the pure movement the body becomes alive and communicative.*

Articulation exercises for different parts of the body

In speech and linguistics, articulation refers to the act of forming sound with the mouth, lips, tongue and other organs. In movement, articulation refers to the act of developing a body which has the ability to respond accurately to thought and imagination. To achieve this, one of the most valuable ways is by breaking down movement into component parts, or isolation exercises. The exercises encourage muscular awareness and control, and increase the range of expressive possibilities.

Differentiating the separate body parts and clarifying the relationship between those parts develops the economy of movement which frees the performer to control the space around them. It is an important feature in training actors because it allows detail to be given to one part of the body at a time, before bringing the body back to a whole. Sometimes it is helpful to break down a movement or give attention to just one part of the body, so that it is less confusing for the student when trying a difficult movement.

These exercises will help different parts of the body to achieve the universal state. Most of the movement work starts with parallel feet so the student will begin the process of alignment and neutrality. Once the actor can function, he can move the body to more profound imaginative work.

The stance: parallel feet

When it is hard for a student to stand with feet parallel without the bottom protruding and the knees knocking, there are certain exercises you can do to encourage the legs into the right position.

1. Stand with feet parallel and then squeeze the bottom really hard, locking the knees out and feeling as if the hips are being turned right out with the right hip facing right and the left hip facing left. Then release the knees quickly.
2. Pelvic rocking. Rock the pelvis under and back, under and back, with the knees released and the pelvis swinging like a boat. Place the palms of the hands on the front joint between the thighs and the torso so the hips flatten and fill the hands when the pelvis rocks under, and then empties the palms when it rocks back.
3. After rocking for a few times the student should end up with their palms filled. Stay there and then very carefully extend the legs and release the knees.
4. The legs will then feel quite strong and the pelvic floor will be lifted in the body, allowing better vocal support. With practice, this exercise will encourage the tail bone to lengthen and the pelvis to open and flatten in the front, allowing the feet to be in parallel with the knees over the toes.

Feet

The feet are important not only because they support the body but because they are expressive in themselves. As soon as an actor puts on a pair of shoes they change the way they stand, act and speak. Wearing a pair of bright red stiletto heels with pointed toes will make the actor feel very different from when they wear a pair of Doctor Martins. When training stage actors are most usually in bare feet. When they have really got back in touch with the natural foot, shoes may be introduced and it is important that the shoes should be appropriate for any character that the actor wishes to portray.

Footwork standing

Teaching point

Be aware, some actors in training can find these exercises make them feel nauseous, especially if it is the first time they have worked in bare feet.

1. Stand with the feet parallel, spine lengthened and neck and head free.

2. Lift the heel of one foot off the floor, pushing the arch up with the weight on the ball of the foot.

3. Extend the toes off the floor in a flicking position, stretching the toes hard.

4. Place the ball of the foot back down on the floor.

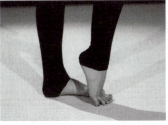

5. Place the heel back down on the floor.
6. Repeat on the other foot.
7. Bend both knees forward as far as you can go without lifting the heels off the floor.
8. Lift the heels off, pushing over into the balls of the feet.
9. Stretch out knees until you are high up onto the balls of the feet.
10. Place the heels back down on the floor.
11. Repeat eight times and then reverse the process (12–15).
12. Rise high up onto the balls of the feet.
13. Bend the knees.
14. Place the heels down on the floor keeping the knees bent.
15. Stretch the knees.

Footwork (sitting)

1. Sit with the legs out in front of you and your hands down next to you. Using only the muscles in your legs, pull back the whole foot until the heels pop off the floor.
2. Stretch the feet back down towards the floor.
3. Lift only the foot (leaving the toes behind) then flick the toes up.
4. Lengthen the whole foot (but not the toes) then finally lengthen the toes.
5. Speed this up and you have undulation of the foot.
6. Repeat it the other way by stretching the feet to the floor to start with and then pull only the toes back.
7. Pull the whole of the foot back.
8. Stretch down only the toes and then extend the whole foot in a point once again.
9. Keep repeating it and it becomes undulation of the foot in the opposite direction.

During many of the movement exercises and the period dance work, the student must understand the different feet and leg positions. The following definitions describe the terminology.

Flat foot

This is when all of the foot is on the ground (not to be confused with flat feet, which is what they are when the arches have dropped and can cause discomfort). The knees are released and this is the usual working stance for an actor.

Sprung foot

This is when the heels are just off the floor and the knees are braced. This is frequently used in period dance, and gives the sense of gliding.

Demi point

This is right up on the balls of the feet, with the weight in between the first and second toes to stop sickling (which is when the actor turns their foot in from the ankle, breaking the straight line of the leg).

Full point

This is needed in ballet, when you go right up onto your toes with aid of a blocked shoe. Actors don't usually need this.

Legs

The legs need releasing and stretching to allow a free, strong walk which enables the actor to change and transform their walk for whatever character they are playing. If they only have a tight, locked walk, this would restrict their choice and possibilities to change.

Locked knees

This is when the knees are pulled back at the joint accentuating the thigh muscles and squeezing the buttocks hard. When the knees are in this state, they are very good for stretching, building strength and gymnastic or balletic movement but will undoubtedly lock the jaw and cause tension in the speaking voice.

Braced knees

This is when the thigh is pulled up with the muscles engaged but the joint is not pulled back. It is the state the knees are in for some dance styles, more released stretching and some occasions in acting where the actor needs tension but must not trap the breath.

Released knees

Released knees are when the knee caps are loose and the joints are bent, but not floppy. Actors need released knees the most, as when they are in this position the jaw can stay free as well as the breath.

Bent knees

Bent knees are when the joints are bent outwards; the opposite of locked. Bent knees can be as a much of a problem as locked knees as they can make the actor very tense. The actor in training can mistake 'bent' for 'released'.

To illustrate the difference between the above states try the following exercise:

1. Squeeze every muscle in your body: the knees, the bottom, the thighs, the tummy, and finally stretch the arms as high as they will go.
2. Now say this: 'The rain in Spain falls mainly on the plain' (or a longer sentence). You will find your voice becomes squeaky and the jaw tense, and you can't breathe or move.
3. Now let everything go. Release everything. Arms. Tummy. Thighs. Bottom. Knees.

Now repeat the sentence again. The breath becomes free and the voice resonant.

4. Try bending the knees hard and walk around the space. Note how funny everybody looks and how impossible it is to walk properly. Of course, you may have to play a character where these contortions are entirely appropriate.

The head and face

It is important to work the face, tongue and scalp, to allow good articulation in speech.

1. Start by chewing with every part of the face and head. Chew with large slow movements and then speed them up until they become quick, rapid.
2. Next, take the hands and massage gently, in small circular movements, all over the face, neck and top of the head.
3. Stick out the tongue and move it round and round, up and down, and as if you are licking an enormous ice cream.
4. Gently tap all over the face and head.
5. Massage your head or face yourself or get someone else to do it.

The head and neck

Exercise 1

1. Lie down on the back, semi-supine.[2]
2. Move the head from right to left, firstly dropping it heavily and then speeding it up.
3. Nod the head heavily up and down, unlocking the jaw and keeping it free.
4. Lift the head off the floor and put the chin on the chest, stretching the neck.
5. Put your head back on the floor and then look to the back wall, opening the throat.
6. Repeat several times.
7. Make a circular movement with the head, unlocking the jaw and keeping the tongue soft.
8. Repeat in the opposite direction.

Exercise 2

1. Go onto all fours, with your knees, hip width apart and your hands, shoulder width apart.
2. Circle the head and neck round and round, opening the throat and letting the jaw drop open.
3. Keep the face released.
4. Stand up.
5. Drop the head forward.
6. Take the head slowly round to the left and drop it down again and roll it round to the right. Keep the jaw released and the mouth loose.

Undulations

Undulations work through the spine, rather like a snake. If the spine and body can spiral and undulate then it allows an articulate transformation of character.

Once the students can master a fluid undulation then try stopping in different parts of the body and see what type of person would have a body shape like that. Build a character around that shape. Of course the undulations need a lot of practice before the student is able to use one part of their body for character purposes. If it has not been practised until fluid and articulate then it will be stiff and unnatural.

---

[2] Supine comes from Latin and means to lie flat on one's back. In the semi-supine position, the person lies on their back but with the knees bent. It is specific term of the Alexander Technique.

Preparation for undulations

1. Sit on the floor, knees bent, facing the ceiling, and feet flat on the floor.
2. Place the hands around the knees and keep the back straight.
3. Curve the back and follow through with the head. Push the bottom of the back up and lengthen the spine.
4. Repeat several times until the bottom of the back really gets moving and then curve it, lengthen it up and undulate the spine, up and over the knees like a wave.

Undulations against the wall

1. Start with your spine flat against the wall, the feet away from the wall, hip width apart, and the knees slightly bent.
2. Wriggle the spine against the wall, making sure the tummy is soft and the back and shoulders are in contact with the wall.
3. Bend and straighten the knees, bending and pushing the thighs forward. Peel each vertebra away from the wall, right up to the neck. Then, reverse, pressing each vertebra into the wall, one by one, until the body is back in the original position.
4. Repeat several times, then push yourself off the wall and feel your body; planting your feet, releasing your knees. The feeling in the spine is very live and stimulated from working against the wall.

Undulations in the space

1. Stand with the feet just wider than hip width apart.
2. Point your finger out in front of you with an outstretched arm, as if pointing to a fly on the wall.
3. The fly then flies down to the floor, up to your knees, crotch, tummy button, chest, neck, head, over the back wall and then down on the floor.
4. The body responds accordingly. The upper body leans forward and releases the knees.
5. As the fly comes to the knees they release further, then the thighs push forward, then the pelvis and up to the tummy, chest and neck and head and off the top of the head and then fall forward again to the beginning posture. You can then ripple this through and up and over, progressing to doing it without the pointed finger.

Full circle earth to sky

1. Stand with the feet wider than the hips and draw a big circle in front of you with your pointing finger. Draw it down to the floor and then up your crotch and up your front and over your chest and right back over your head in a massive back bend, up to the sky and back in front of you.
2. Respond with your body in a huge undulation.

Shoulders and sternum

Shoulders and sternum (standing)

1. Stand with the feet hip width apart.
2. Let the right arm float up, palm facing the front, extended, but not tense or locked, energy travelling through like a bird's wing.

3. Let it drop heavily to your side so that the shoulder releases, as with an arm swing (see p. 51).
4. Repeat with the left arm.
5. Take the right arm out, in the same manner as before, and start curling the arm in like a long spiral, from the finger tips all the way through your arm until you reach your shoulder. Keep the head up to start with so you really can feel the spiral stretch through the arm and the shoulder.
6. Repeat with the left arm.
7. Next take the tension out of the exercise and feel as if your hands are curling in like a lotus flower. Release the breath and release into the sternum. But no lower. Release the knees at the end of the breath.
8. Have the image of the light going out of your face and body to a rather depressed pose and then the light entering the body and face, up and out into the universe with positivity.
9. Repeat with the left arm.
10. Repeat with both arms together.
11. Now travel. It is very difficult to keep the walking smoothly and to use the arms in this way.

You can make up anything you like, but a tried and tested version is:

Curl in, 2, 3, 4 (as you simultaneously walk 2, 3, 4) and curl out 2, 3, 4 (as you simultaneously walk 2, 3, 4) take the arms up 2, 3, 4 (as if you are appealing to the gods) and bring them down 2, 3, 4 as if you are coming back to your centre. Really make sure that all the time the legs are loose and the work is being located in the upper spine and shoulders and sternum.

Get into pairs across the space from each other. Repeat the exercise towards and away from each other using walking forward and backwards.

Upper body (standing)
1. Clasp your arms around your body, tight like a straight jacket.
2. Move the upper body from right to left in a huge swinging motion.
3. Start walking, swinging the body as you go. (This feels very funny, but once you let go the upper body feels very loose and free.)

Upper body arms and shoulders (supine)
1. Lie semi-supine, feet just a little wider than your hips, arms open wide, palms facing the ceiling.
2. Lift the arms an inch (or a couple of centimetres) off the floor. Keep the wrists loose and the fingers soft. Hold for a couple of seconds then lower to the ground. Feel the weight through the body and arms. Imagine that your arms are going on forever or that you are holding a big long pole.
3. Slowly (to 40 counts) take the arms up towards each other until your palms are facing each other, not touching, just feel the heat of your hands.
4. Stretch your shoulders off the floor and drop them back down to the ground, reaching up with your fingers with open hands, keeping the elbows extended, but not locked
5. Drop your shoulders back down into the ground.
6. Repeat a few times as desired and then turn your palms to face the front and take your arms back over

your head slowly for 40 counts again. (Make sure you encourage the centre of your body to the ground. At this point if you have stiff shoulders, you need to be very careful. Try and keep your arms extended but if you can't then release your elbows or do not go down so low.)

7. Stay there and breathe.
8. Lift the arms back up again for another 40 counts.
9. Lift the shoulders up and down from the floor and then open them out to the first position.

Variations

When the arms are up in the air, twist them from the shoulder as if you are going to unscrew a light bulb, let your neck and head be released and your jaw unlocked.

You can do this with a partner. One person stands over the other and lifts the arms from the wrists and pulls the shoulders up and down off the floor and then pulls the arms out and down above the head.

Arms and shoulders (supine)

Exercise 1

1. Lie semi-supine on the floor, legs hip width apart and knees floating to the ceiling, arms down by your side and the palms facing the floor.
2. Lift your arms in parallel, over your head to behind you.
3. Bring them back down next to you (check that the centre of your back is against the floor and that you are lengthening and widening your back).
4. Now start breathing in as your arms go over your head and out as they come back down again.
5. Slow your breath and really synchronise your breath and movement.

Exercise 2

1. Lie semi-supine, arms down by your side, palms facing the ceiling, the back of your middle finger stretched out against the floor.
2. Sweep the backs of the hands along the floor to above your head and then back down again.
3. Repeat several times, making sure you are encouraging your lower back to be in contact with the floor.

Spine

The spine sustains the entire body. We need to be aware of each section of the spine and its relationship to the whole body.

Exercise 1

1. Close your eyes.
2. Focus your attention on the spine. Think of each vertebra resting on top of the next one in a long jointed column.
3. Starting from the top of the spine, let the head slowly drop forward leaving the arms and shoulders loose. (Allow the weight of the head to pull the spine downwards, vertebra by vertebra, until hanging head downwards from the hips.)

4. Do not keep the knees straight. Allow them to relax as and when necessary as you drop through your spine.
5. Uncurl, slowly building each vertebra up on top of the one below, starting from the base of the spine. Think of them as small building blocks.
6. Carry on until standing upright leaving the head last.
7. Allow the head to rest lightly on top of the spinal column. Think of the column continuing up beyond the top of the head.
8. Leave the arms and shoulders relaxed and passive throughout the exercise.
9. Repeat with a partner pressing with their fingertips on each vertebra in turn to increase the awareness of the process. The partner should check if the shoulders and arms are hanging loosely, as well as making sure the head is left until last.

Exercise 2

1. Work in pairs; one person stands as neutral as possible and their partner stands behind them.
2. The partner standing behind will massage their way down the spine from the neck, vertebra by vertebra. As the part of the spine is massaged (actually between the bones), the person will roll forward until they touch the floor with their fingertips, with their bottom in the air, knees released, knees directed over the centre of the toes.
3. The partner then pushes their neck, carefully so that the head is free and the neck is released and then they gently bounce the upper spine and the shoulders so that they are loose and free.
4. They then work up from the bottom of the spine rolling back up again to standing, body aligned arms hanging freely by the sides and spine stacked up on top of itself. The student should be able to notice how the body feels floating released and the voice free.

Exercise 3 – Arching and rounding

1. On hands and knees on the floor (place the hands directly below the shoulders and the knees below the hips creating right angles. Make sure the weight is evenly distributed through the hands and feet), arch the spine downwards like a cat stretching.
2. Then push the spine towards the ceiling to reverse the position; this is called 'round'.
3. Repeat eight times. Do this very slowly trying not to engage the stomach muscles. This will seem impossible at first in the 'round' position. Try to breathe into the belly in both positions and keep the head as free as possible. Try to keep the spine long throughout the exercise. In the arched position avoid crushing or squashing the upper vertebrae and try not to sink into it but lengthen forwards and upwards.

Variations: pelvic thrust

Try to make the movement starting at the base of the spine and rippling through to the neck. Do this in both directions. Think of each vertebra separately in the lowering of the spine in the 'pelvic thrust', but this time the movement starts at the base of the spine. Don't hurry; try to experience this through the whole spine.

In the 'arch' position, extend the right leg backwards in air as high as possible without straining. Bring the knee in towards head and replace on floor. Repeat with left leg. Check breathing while leg is lifted in the air.

Variation with partner

- One person is on all fours and the other walks their fingers up the spine, vertebrae by vertebrae, and the spine responds by curling under into the round position, really making sure the spine is working part by part. If the spine is in any way locked (stiff) at any particular point up and down the spine, then this exercise will help limber up that part of the spine which needs to loosen.
- Repeat from the bottom of the spine, this time arching. Keep repeating a few times before doing it on your own with the physical memory, and the spine will look like a wave or a snake undulating.
- Swap partners.
- Repeat starting from the neck and work down the spine to the tail bone.

Sea serpent (DVD: Exercise 6)

1. Start in neutral and then bring the arms up the front of the body until they are reaching above the head.
2. Keeping the arms next to the ears, imagine that the hands are now the eyes.
3. Curl down through the spine all the way to the bottom (release the knees). Look around the bottom of the sea with the new eyes.
4. Arch up, keeping the legs bent and the arms by the ears.
5. Lengthen up in the centre of the spine and look around at the top of the movement with the hands for eyes.

Spine and shoulders

Back arches exercise (camel)

1. Kneel down with your knees hip width apart.
2. Lift your arms up the front of your body and open your arms and then place your hands on your heels, gripping them tight.
3. Push your hips far forward and let the head drop back, looking at the wall behind you.

Upper spine exercise

1. Stand in the neutral or central stance.
2. Point your finger at your chest. Shrink away from it until the chest is concave. This will look like a person who is feeling depressed.
3. Now imagine a finger is pointing between your shoulder blades. Shrink away from it by pushing the spine forward so that the upper spine is arched and the chest is convex. Come back to your normal stance.

4. Repeat this without actually pointing your finger and coming into your normal stance between each position (normal, concave, normal, convex, normal, etc.). During this exercise avoid arching or rounding the small of your back. Keep it isolated from the upper back.

⊙ Arching and rounding the spine exercise (bear and bird) (DVD: Exercise 7)

1. Begin in neutral or central stance.
2. Release the knees and bring both arms forward in line with the chest, rounding the spine to create a C shape with the pelvis scooped under. (The head remains in line with the spine and arms are positioned as if embracing a ball.)
3. Release the knees and allow the pelvis to tilt forward, with spine following to create an arch in the back. Simultaneously open the arms out to the side so your whole spine and rib cage arches in space. (The arms are positioned slightly below shoulder height with palms facing forwards and elbows are soft, not locked.)
4. Release the knees and allow the tail bone to curl under you once more with the spine following the impulse into a rounded C shape as before. The arms simultaneously float out and forward to embrace the huge ball.
5. Repeat eight times.

Bear and bird – a Trish Arnold exercise
In the C shaped body, the arms are like the forelegs of a standing bear embracing a large sphere or globe. As the back arches, the arms are like a bird's wings, as it flaps them on the ground, or as they seem to be exercising them.

During this sequence of movements, find how you can initiate the movement from the knees and the base of the spine. Also, find a quality of fluidity: gently rocking, not jerking. Experiment with released easy breathing, as this will help you discover the feeling of fluidity and ease.

Extra stretches for ribs and spine

1. Begin in a central position, feet wider than hip distance apart. Knees soft, arms hanging freely by the side.
2. Release the knees and lift the right arm out to the right over your head as if you were trying to sweep the ceiling. Stay flat or on the frontal plane. Take the weight onto your left leg and bend the knee leaving the right leg straight.

3. Continue the stretch to the left by bending sideways at the waist and reaching as far to the side as possible (keep breathing into the stretch).
4. Let the right arm fall and swing around to its natural position by your side as you transfer the weight to the centre, releasing the head and sternum slightly forward and then come up to the right.
5. Repeat with your left arm.

This is simply another variation of a rib stretch but also really engages the leg muscles.

Don't hold a stretch in a fixed position; allow the breath to find fluidity in motion, gently encouraging the body to expand and release rather than forcing it. This enables the breath to work in and out of the body freely.

> **Teaching tip**
>
> *This is a very dramatic movement which is rather strenuous on the back and knees, so make sure that you only do it when you are warmed up. You can do smaller versions if you are stiff.*

Bridges

1. Lie down on the floor, semi-supine.
2. Release the bottom of the spine into the floor. Imagine there is a string at the base of the spine that is being pulled up towards the ceiling. Each vertebra should lift off the floor one by one, right up to the neck. You want to feel each vertebra rise from the floor, but without muscular tension; try using the image of a piece of velvet satin being lifted gently, and then laid down gently. The spine should be free and released, and the strength is placed in the thighs, shins and calves.
3. Roll up and down in this position several times.
4. Next, take your arms over your head and repeat the exercise.
5. Then add your hands, by your ears, and push up into a high bridge.

> **Teaching point**
>
> *This is quite an advanced movement for some people, particularly adults, so you need to build up the suppleness and strength in the back.*
>
> *For adults, particularly men, it is best to stretch the arch into the shoulders and upper spine rather than the middle of the back. It stops the strain in the lower back, and doubles up as a great opener for the upper torso and sternum, which often need a good stretch the other way, due to upper body building or just general stooping forward.*

Demi-cobra and cobra

1. Lie on your tummy, arms down by your side.
2. Lift the upper body and then lower it (repeat as many times as you wish).
3. Lift the upper body and place your hands by your shoulders on the floor, lifting your body up further.

Teaching point

If there is pain in the lower back, then do not go so high. As each body is different, try experimenting with arm positions. Firstly, try with the arms close to the body, then secondly with the elbows floating out to the side. Both are useful, and if one is uncomfortable for the spine, then try the other one.

Remember, stretching is good, but pain is not!

Pelvis

It is very important for the pelvis to be free and released. If it is tense and locked then it does not allow the actor to walk in a free way. It also blocks the breath and is unaccommodating for the voice. The pelvis links the legs and the torso, and helps to support a free, strong, standing position as well as a released walk.

Pelvic rock (standing)

1. Begin in the central stance, feet slightly wider than the hips. Knees directed over the first toe.
2. Release the knees and tip the pelvis forward, creating an arch in the lower spine. (Only the lower back is active. The rest of the spine stays passive.)
3. Straighten the legs slightly then release the knees twice making two small bouncing motions. On the second bounce, roll the pelvis under flattening the small of the back.
4. Bounce twice again and release the pelvis on the second bounce creating an arch in the lower spine once more. Repeat as often as desired.

The pelvis should swing or rock as if it is a boat or a swing. The lower back and waist are engaged. The upper back and shoulders stay passive. To help keep the upper body still, place hands on the head. Progress this exercise to swinging the pelvis, under and out on each bounce. Make a dance movement with the hips and pelvis, under and out, with released knees and bouncing movement. Knees very active and soft and always lead with movement in the spine.

Imagine that the pelvis is a basin. In the basin there is some mayonnaise. While doing this exercise, imagine that you are not going to allow the mayonnaise to go over the edge of the basin. This image should keep the student from becoming tense and locked, stopping the breath and gritting the teeth.

Samba pelvis

1. Swing the pelvis in a circle with loose knees. This time imagine your pelvis is controlling a spoon, and you need to stir a basin of mayonnaise with a smooth, gentle motion.
2. Combine swinging under and out with circling.
3. Figure of eight with the pelvis.
4. Shake the bottom as hard and as isolated from the rest of the body as possible.

Pelvic rock (semi-supine) or clock face

1. Lie semi-supine, feet a little wider than hip width apart.
2. Imagine that you are lying with the base of your spine in the centre of a clock face, your belly button is 12 o'clock, under the base of the spine is 6 o'clock, the left hip is 3 o'clock and the right hip is 9 o'clock.
3. Keeping your legs as loose as possible, i.e. no tension in your thighs, tilt your pelvis up to 12 o'clock.
4. Tip it down to 6 o'clock.
5. Tip it right to 9 o'clock and left to 3 o'clock.
6. Repeat several times.
7. Then start pelvic rocking, like your own private jelly, wobble 12 o'clock to 6 o'clock, up, down, up, down, up, down.
8. Now do this from side to side, letting the knees release a little, so it also feels a bit like a massage to the lower back. It really begins to open your pelvis.
9. Then go round and round the clock face 12, 1, 2, 3, 4, 5, 6, 7, 8, 9, 10, 11.
10. Then round and round anti-clock wise.

Variation of pelvic rock (semi-supine)

- Work in pairs, A and B. A sits at the bottom of B's feet and puts their hands on B's thighs.
- When B drops his pelvis to 12 on the clock face hold gently.
- When B drops to 6 pull on the thighs.
- Repeat to 3 and 9.

Teaching points

It should be possible to pelvic rock for a long time without getting tired. However, if the student's back arches it may help to lie down with legs stretched out in front and rock the pelvis up and down. When the student gets up the positive effects on voice and posture are enormous.

Always get the student up on their feet to notice the difference in their posture.

Floor exercises for the spine
Pelvic thrust

1. Lie on your back in the semi-supine position with heels as close as possible to the buttocks, slightly further apart than the hips, knees to the ceiling.
2. Breathe in and out; as the breath leaves the body thrust the pelvis towards the ceiling as high as possible. Put the hands on your buttocks and push a little higher so that there is maximum arch of the spine.
3. Place the hands on the floor. The weight is now being carried on the feet and shoulders and the thighs are strongly engaged in supporting the weight of the pelvis. Check that you are not holding your breath, and that you are breathing naturally.
4. Keeping the breathing easy, start to lower the spine to the floor, vertebra by vertebra, starting at the point nearest to the neck and finishing as near to the base of the spine as possible. Do not worry if this cannot be carried out literally, it is an image to help the spine be active.

5. The spine should feel very long when it has returned to the floor. Think of it reaching to the heels. Release all joints and breath.

6. Adjust the feet if necessary and repeat three more times.

Teaching point

Feet, although not parallel, should not be very divergent, as this will prevent the correct engagement of the thighs.

Variation 1

○ Place your arms beyond your head on the floor.

○ Breathe in and out and as the breath leaves the body thrust the pelvis towards the ceiling as high as possible. Leave the arms above the head whilst returning the pelvis to the floor. This gives a big extension to the rib cage.

○ Always release after the action and keep the breath going steadily throughout the movement of the spine.

Variation 2

○ Take the base of the spine off the floor and make very small circles with the pelvis.

○ Lower the bottom of the spine back to the floor.

○ Build up vertebra by vertebra until every part of the spine has had an internal circling therefore being massaged and lengthened.

Spinal twist

1. Lie semi-supine.
2. Pull your left heel into your lower spine, with your foot as close to the base of your spine as possible.
3. Cross your right leg all the way over as if sitting with your legs crossed in a chair.
4. Open the arms out to the side, look to the left.
5. Drop the legs to the right and let them bounce back up.
6. Repeat down to the left.
7. Change the legs so the other one is on the top and repeat the stretching motion.

This can be quite strenuous on the knees and the back, so make sure the student is careful. If they feel any pain, they should stop this exercise.

Hip circles

1. Lie semi-supine.
2. Take the knees into your hands, making sure that your hands are doing all the work so that your pelvis can be loose.

3. First, let your knees drop wide open. (For an extra stretch and opening of the pelvis, you can lower your chin onto your chest. This is a real opener for the pelvis as it is one of the classic positions to give birth in!)
4. When you have stretched the legs wide, circle the legs gently outwards in their sockets as if you are stirring two spoons in a basin (the pelvis) of mayonnaise.
5. Repeat, bringing the legs in towards each other.
6. Move them all over the place, really trying to keep the tension out of the pelvis.
7. Repeat the stirring with the legs together.

If the arms get tired because the legs are heavy, then the students should allow their legs to drop into semi-supine again. It is more important that the pelvis is loose and that the student is genuinely using their arms and hands, than it is to make the general shape. If the student has difficulty letting go the control of their legs, then the exercise could be done in pairs; one student lies semi-supine and remains as relaxed as possible while the partner lifts their legs and moves them round in the sockets.

Keep rocking forward and back, forward and back, making sure to release the knees, jaw and breath.

Stir the pelvis round and round in circles first one way and then the other.

Make a figure of eight with the pelvis, like a salsa dance.

Part 2

Movements with imagination at the heart of pure movement

5 Core movement exercises

The following movement exercises are the basis of the pure movement work. They are taught throughout a three year training course as warm ups for individuals or groups.[video and photos]

Rib stretches

It is usual to start with rib stretches. It is therefore important to find the natural yawn and stretch, taking the impulse from the yawn. The students imitate this action.

A stretch is like a yawn in that it always starts with the impulse of a breath. Do not force the energy, start from where you are in the yawn and let it spread through your arms, spine, neck, rib cage, shoulders, wrists and ankles. Repeat two or three times, making it a new experience every time you do it. Keep the yawn natural. A good stretch is elastic; the body expands and expands, and is then released. It never becomes a held position.

Try yawning and stretching at the same time thinking 'breathe, stretch, give in', then repeat and say the words out loud.

Use the space all around you: above your head, behind you, below the waist and knees, to the side, and forward.

NB DVD for rib stretches will have four of each.

The rib stretches have not only an impulsive, natural element to them, but they also have a technical element. The following exercises describe technique in detail.

⊙ High rib stretch (DVD: Exercises 8 & 9)

1. Begin in a central stance (see neutral or universal, p. 24), feet slightly more than hip width apart, and knees soft and not locked, arms hanging freely by sides and feet directed forward.
2. Let the knees give a little and collapse the chest, drop the head into a depressed position.
3. Take a deep breath and transfer the weight over onto the right leg, keeping the left foot 'empty' or released.

4. Using the memory of a real yawn, use the impulse of it to stretch the right arm above the head. The ribs should be stretched like a concertina, and you should feel as if you are being stretched in two directions, by the arm to the ceiling, and by the leg and foot down through the floor, transferring weight onto the right foot as you do so. The knee of the supporting leg is braced at the end of the movement. Do not rise onto your toes. In fact, imagine that your feet are the roots of a tree growing deep into the earth. The end of the movement should look as if you have reached as high as you can, the right side of the rib cage should be bulging outwards.

5. Collapse to the centre, releasing into the sternum.

6. Repeat to the left, and keep on repeating right and left, as often as desired.

Teaching point

The student should notice the difference in the physical sensation between the collapsed and the extended body. This physicality can also provoke different emotions. Encourage the students to focus on using the image of the back of the rib cage and keeping the back and chest broad; this will help them to stay on the frontal plain without twisting the torso. It is important to keep the spine long and the pelvis in the neutral position, not tilted backwards or forwards. It is especially important not to lift the chin and crush the cervical spine.

For this and all following exercises, the knees must remain directly over the feet.

Teaching point

As well as the technical work, the teacher needs to feed in imaginative images, such as: 'You are reaching for the sun or the moon'. The students should let the image affect their body.

🖭 Side or wide rib stretch (DVD: Exercises 8 & 9)

1. Begin in the central, neutral or universal stance with feet wider apart than for the high rib stretch. Knees released, arms hanging loosely by your sides.
2. Stretch your right arm out to the side taking the weight onto your right leg (sideways lunge). The impulse is from the ribcage through the elbow, hand and fingers opening the right ribs.
3. When you have reached the end of the movement, release the right arm allowing the head and torso to fall over to the right slightly. Simultaneously begin to reach out to the opposite side with the left arm, the impulse coming from the left ribs and transfer the weight through the central stance and onto your left leg.
4. Continue from side to side like a wave as if you are wading through water.

Important

○ Throughout the movement remain facing the front on the lateral plane. Do not fall or twist into forward space, as this will distort the exercise.

○ The impulse for the movement, as with all the rib stretches, is from the ribcage itself.

○ This exercise engages the ribs on the side you are reaching towards, encouraging openness and ease of motion to support the breath and consequently the voice.

○ When you've reached it, don't hold onto the extension. Let it go and continue with an new impulse.

⊛ Forward rib stretch (DVD: Exercises 8 & 9)

1. Begin in the central, neutral or universal stance, as before, with the feet wider than hip distance apart.
2. Stretch forward with the right arm initiating the movement from the lower back and ribs through the shoulder, elbow and hand.
3. As you reach forward transfer the weight onto the right bent leg. The left leg is straight. The head stays in line with the spine so it is dropped a little under the stretching arm. The spine is rounded slightly forming a C shape.
4. When you have reached to the full extension release your right arm so it hangs naturally at your side.
5. Reach your left arm forward, again with the image of the impulse from the back of the rib cage as you transfer the weight through the central stance onto your left bent leg with the right leg straight at the end of the journey.
6. Repeat as often as desired.

Variation

- Work in pairs.
- One person starts the rib stretch (as described above), and the other places their hands on either side of their partner's ribs, sweeping their hands up the rib cage and through the hands. This gives an extra stretch, enabling the movement to be performed more fully than when executed in isolation.

⊛ Shaking down through the spine with bounces (DVD: Exercise 10)

The benefits of this exercise are to loosen and lengthen the spine and to start gentle stretching for the backs of the legs and the back. When you return to the standing position then your posture is more lengthened.

1. Begin with a central stance. Release the knees and lengthen again in a gentle bouncing motion, keeping the body erect and the arms hanging loosely by your sides.
2. With each bounce allow your head and torso to drop forward until you are hanging off the spine with legs still lengthened. Continue to bounce the knees loosely leaving the arms and head hanging freely off the spine.
3. With each bounce come up to the central stance.

Here is an example of a routine of shaking down through the spine with bounces

- eight counts to bounce the knees;
- eight counts to drop the head forward whilst bouncing the knees;
- eight counts to drop over to the centre of spine whilst bouncing the knees;

- eight counts all the way down the spine, bottom in the air;
- eight counts to shake out the body and knees;
- eight counts to roll up smoothly through the spine.

Repeat the exercise on the count of four, then the count of two, then the count of one. It is very difficult to remain free and released on the count of one, but it can cause a lot of mirth, and eventually huge satisfaction when the students can simultaneously move freely, intricately and quickly. These shake-downs and bounces can be repeated with the same counting over to the right side and the left side of the body.

Teaching point

The benefits of using these numbers of bounces are that they are regular and there are enough to open the spine, but not too many to make the student dizzy. It keeps the exercise rhythmic and fun when teaching large numbers of people. It also engages the student's brain as well as body.

Swings (part of pure movement)

In actor training, the arm swings are designed with a functional consideration to:

- stimulate the release of excess tension in the muscles in the surrounding area, i.e. the intercostal muscles of the rib cage;
- engage and stimulate the movement of the shoulders and ribs to encourage free released motion (unrestricted movement): minimising excess tension allows more space for breath to flow freely through the body enabling the lungs and diaphragm to work to their full capacity without restriction and provide maximum support for the voice;
- promote a freedom and ease in movement and stimulate the flow of energy throughout the body.

Like rib stretches, the swings offer immeasurable benefits to actor training. For any actor, the process of learning the swings is not as easy as one might imagine. To achieve the maximum effect of a swing, you must surrender your body to the gravitational force that surrounds us, enabling a true discovery of the weight of the arm, body or legs, depending on the particular swing that is being tackled. Only then can we achieve the pendulum motion that will stimulate muscular release and create the opportunity for expression. The journey of the swing must involve a drop, a total release, and a moment of suspension. If the free flow of the swing is stopped or held at any moment then it is impossible to experience the weight of the arm (torso or legs) as the body is engaging in unnecessary tension. The absolute sense of freedom that can be experienced when a true swing is achieved is exhilarating and I believe that this exhilaration will take the actor to a greater level of creativity. The swings embrace many aspects raised by the rib stretches; use of space, direction and dimensions. The actor must unlock their creative imagination and allow the movement of the swing to travel through space, to own the space and find the expressive nature of the journey. The release of excess tension in the body through movement can create powerful emotions; a swing can generate a sense of elation if performed with dexterity.

It is really important to encourage actors to travel through space with an arm swing; an actor can gallop across a room allowing the momentum of the swing to motivate the journey. When one plays with the expansiveness of the movement and the ease with which the body moves through space, the expressive imagination reveals itself. The moment of suspension required when a swing reaches its highest point is difficult to achieve, but absolutely necessary. It can be related to text. For example, the renowned 'Pinter pauses'. These pauses or beats are not full stops; they are moments of suspension, the energy flow of the language and atmosphere is dramatically suspended. If an actor stops this flow then the energy is dropped and the dramatic tension of the scenario lost. It is therefore apparent that not only are the physical and expressive benefits of the swings significant but their role in actor training goes further. This is a prime example of the way movement classes can interact with other elements of the actor training, and can provide useful insights into text and performance.

Teaching points

Swinging is a simple concept but can be difficult to achieve. Imagery can be used to help swinging, such as: 'Think of a child's swing. Imagine you are on it. Remember the feeling of it dropping with gravity at the bottom and the moment of suspension at the top, before it drops back down again'. It is possible for the student to hold a heavy object as they learn to swing as it gives them the feeling of gravity, weight and suspension.

Swings work on several levels. Firstly, the body becomes freer, more released and much stronger. Secondly, they allow the body to find weight and suspension, and thirdly they enable the body to travel in space on every level.

Exercises to aid a swing
To find the weight and release in the arms.

1. Get into pairs, A and B. A stands on two feet as perfectly balanced as possible (A can then shut their eyes if that help them release).
2. B takes hold of one of A's arms and moves it around in its socket and joints.
3. B then shakes it gently and tries to find a release.
4. B then does the same with the other arm.
5. B takes the arms underneath the elbows and lifts and drops them, floppy like a rag doll.

Taking the arm up
This exercise will allow the students to find the floating sensation when the arms go up through space in preparation for the arm swing.

1. Stand next to a wall, with a strong firm stance (see stance, p. 28).
2. Press the back of the arm which is nearest to the wall, very hard with all of your weight behind it for a minute.

3. Step away from the wall and watch the arm float up into the air. You will find it floats up on its own without muscular tension and lifting of the shoulder.
4. Practise recreating the float without the pressure of the wall.

Arm swings

1. Begin in the central stance, feet slightly wider than hip distance apart.
2. Raise the right arm up and out to the side, slightly above shoulder level.
3. Release the arm allowing it to swing across your chest, then swing back to return to its original position. Keep the upper body strong and centred, as if between two planes of glass.
4. Repeat as often as desired then with the left arm.
5. Include full circle swings.

Variations

○ Keep the upper body strong and centred as above.
○ As you swing your right arm across your body, allow your weight to transfer onto your left leg; transfer your weight onto your right leg as you swing to the right.
○ Allow the upper body to respond to the swings, twisting your shoulders and sternum in the direction of the swing. This will take you off centre and away from the panes of glass.
○ Add full circle swings and a change of direction.
○ Allow the head and the sternum to release on the drop of each swing returning to the upright position at the full height of the swing.
○ Swing with balances at suspension points as follows:
   ■ swing the right arm across the chest and back with the weight centred and the body strong;
   ■ continue with a full circle swing;
   ■ at the end of the full circle allow the right arm to continue swinging across your body taking your weight with it into a balance on your left leg;
   ■ drop the weight back into the centre and allow the arm to swing to the open position, back across the body, then full circle ending in a balance on the right leg;
   ■ repeat as often as desired.
○ Play with the suspension of the arm swing and the balance at the same moment.
○ Find the continuation of the swing at its point of suspension in your imagination, the journey continuing forever. This will help you avoid stopping the swing and to find the free flow.
○ Allow the weight of the arm swing to transfer your body weight and the momentum to lift you into the balance.
○ Allow the freedom of the swing to lift your spirits and inspire you.

Ski swing

1. Begin in the central stance, feet hip width apart.
2. Release the knees so they are slightly bent and lean the upper body slightly forward bending from the hips but keeping the spine erect.
3. Raise the right arm up in front of you to shoulder height, keeping the elbow soft and raise your left arm

up behind you to a comfortable height that does not require any lifting of the left shoulder.

4. Swing both your arms forward and backwards at the same time but in different directions i.e. right arm swinging backwards and the left arm swinging forwards. Release the knees on the drop of every swing but do not rotate the upper body.

5. Repeat for eight swings or as often as required.

6. Continue the motion of the arms and allow the momentum of the swing to lift your weight off your heels and onto the balls of your feet. Do not lose your connection with the floor entirely; the balls of your feet remain in contact with the ground. Allow your heels to return to the ground on the drop of every swing so you are bouncing up and down.

7. Repeat for eight swings or as often as required.

8. Continue the motion of the arms and allow the momentum of the swing to take you into a little jump, returning to the ground with the drop of each swing.

9. Repeat for eight swings or as often as required.

Teaching points

*The position of the upper body is very important in the swing. The student must lean forward from the hips and not the waist, keeping the spine as straight as possible. The pelvis must not escape backwards, causing an arch in the lower spine. If the student feels a strain in the lower back, they are probably leaning too far forward. This swing requires a strong spine and should **not** be taught until the students are in their second year of training.*

Find the freedom and weight in the swings as a gorilla does when swinging its arms about.

Try to maintain a forward position with your chest to begin with. Do not allow the upper spine to rotate in the direction of the arm. You can experiment with a rotation of the upper body later but this is not the ski swing. The two variations are of equal benefit; the ski swing will isolate the muscles surrounding the shoulder joint to a greater extent and the swing with rotation will engage more movement of the rib cage.

Play with dimensions; the sense of travelling forward as if skiing down a mountain. Let the freedom of the movement inspire you and this will encourage the release.

Be careful not to let the knees roll in on the landing of the jump. Keep the feet parallel and the knees directly over the toes and below the hips.

Bow and arrow arm swing (DVD: Exercise 11)

1. Stand on a diagonal. Do this by drawing a box around yourself and put your right foot into the top right hand corner and your left foot into the bottom left corner.

2. Let the left arm float up in what should feel like a heroic position.

3. Flop the arm against the body, weight heavy and release the knees but not the spine.

4. Raise the right arm up in front as if aiming for you target.

5. Flop that down and release the knees and not the spine.

6. Take both arms forward, hands together and pull the left arm back to the heroic position and the right arm outstretched.

7. Flop the right arm down, and flop the left arm down. Release the knees on the downward flop.

8. Repeat and look out into the countryside and see your target.

Teaching points

This exercise can be taught in two different patterns: one is to finish the circle where you started it; the other is to finish the circle on the opposite side so that you can start the sequence on alternate sides. The students can then begin shifting their weight from side to side, and can end the exercise by galloping sideways with the momentum of the arm swing.

It is very important to introduce the image of the target and the view over the countryside; these will allow the movement to be dramatically filled with an image, instead of being an empty body movement.

---

9. Next only flop the right arm down and keep the left arm open and heroic.

10. Instead of flopping the left arm down, swing it past the body making sure you find release and weight and suspension at the top.

11. Repeat eight times, making sure not to bend the spine to compensate for any release.

12. The arm just swings forward and back.

13. The head either remains looking at the target or it can follow the arm.

14. Do eight straight and eight following the arm.

☻ Figure of eight arm swing (DVD: Exercise 12)

This is a good exercise for the upper body, shoulders and sternum. It also uses the diagonals and the dimensions of the room.

Preparations for figure of eight arm swing

1. Stand on the diagonal, with the left foot slightly in front of the right. This is easier for beginners.

2. Lift up the right arm up behind the body in the heroic position and then curl down through the fingers, spiralling down the arm until it reaches the shoulder. Release into the sternum. Breathe.

3. Uncurl up from the shoulder, sternum then head and back to the heroic position. Make sure you release into your knees, all the time, and keep the breath natural.

4. Then swing the arm forward through the track of the spiral, but it is now like a traced line and has no tension in it.

5. As the arm comes up to the top, look up in suspension. Turn the palm out, and slap the back of the hand against the thigh, and rebound up.

6. Repeat several times.

7. Repeat all on the left side.

8. Go back to the right arm and swing it down and behind the body making a big curve (the other half of the eight shape).

9. Use the undulation in the lower body (i.e. release the knees forward, into the pelvis and thighs, and up through the spine).

55

10. Join the front half of the eight with the back half of the eight and start swinging.

Teaching point

This can make people feel a little dizzy, so get the students to half close their eyes or to focus on a point in the room as best they can; both these techniques can help.

The swing

1. Stand the central stance with the feet a little wider than the hips and with the feet slightly turned out.
2. Sweep the right arm out and up, as in the heroic position.
3. Using the spiral through the arm and shoulder, drop the arm forward and across your body. Swing it up over your head until it sweeps the sky, palm facing the ceiling.
4. Drop it behind you, opening the palm to the ceiling and swing it behind your body.
5. Release into your knees and then send it back up to the top in the heroic position, where you will find the suspension.
6. Keep swinging forward and up (count 1, 2, 3) and back down behind your body (1, 2, 3) like a waltz.
7. Repeat on the left.

Teaching point

This is a good swing to combine with a travelling motion. In one corner of the room two students form a pair, facing one another using opposite arms. The actors do two figure of eight swings to a count of four, ensuring that their focus is on each other. They then swing the same arm over their head four times as they gallop diagonally across the room. They then stop, balancing their weight on both feet, and repeat the same process right across the room. The use of a large room – or ideally, a big space in the open air – helps this movement to become absolutely exhilarating.

☻ Armswing into armswing and peeping under (DVD: Exercise 13)

1. Face the front.
2. Lean over to the side, imagining the two panes of glass to prevent injury in the back.
3. Reach up diagonally with both arms, high and right. Look under both arms, i.e. 'peeping through', so there is a big sideways stretch. Drop the torso down from the sternum only and swing the body to the left side looking under the arms. During this swing, the knees release at the point where the sternum drops. As the body swings to the left, the weight is transferred onto the left leg, and both knees are braced.

This swing can be executed with one arm or two.

☉ Rag doll swing (DVD: Exercise 14)

This movement works on several levels. Firstly, this is excellent for opening the shoulders, the thoracic spine and the neck. Secondly, the rag doll swing has a powerful syncopated rhythm, which creates a sense of drama.

1. Stand in the central stance, feet a little wider than hip width apart and the feet slightly turned out like a loose second position in ballet.
2. Lift the right arm to shoulder height.
3. Swing it in a full circle in front of the body, keeping the stance straight until the arm has reached the end of the full circle and then drop it on the back of the right leg, left hand against the thigh. At the same time drop the body over to the right on a large bend from the waist.
4. Send the left arm forward across the body on a diagonal, with the impulse from the shoulder, leading with the left hand and swing the body up and drop the arm down by your side, ending back up into the central stance.

Teaching point

Show the students that as soon as the right hand touches the thigh, it sends an immediate impulse to the left shoulder. The student can imagine that they are a floppy rag doll, allowing for further release. It is, however, important to pay attention to the technique and detail. At first the students may become disorientated when performing this swing, and it takes practice to achieve the movement fully.

☉ Broken windmill swing (DVD: Exercise 15)

The students may find this swing difficult at first as it requires complex timing and co-ordination. However, there will be a great feeling of satisfaction when they achieve it, and the rhythm and co-ordination required will be useful when learning more complex moves and dances.

1. Start with feet hip width apart, knees pointing over the toes.
2. Lift the right arm up, palm facing the front.
3. Swing it down towards the thigh and swing it up bending from the elbow, just as it is about to hit into the thigh.
4. Sweep the hand in front of the face as if washing it, then sweep it behind the head as if brushing the hair off the neck.
5. Swing it right up above your head and down and out to the side. Keep repeating it until it is in your body (rhythm: 1 and a 2 and a 3 and a 4)
6. Repeat on the left.
7. Then changing the rhythm co ordinate the two together (and 1 and 2 and 3 and 4).

☻ Discus arm swing (DVD: Exercise 16)

1. Start facing the front, legs a little wider than the hips.
2. Flop the body over to the right side, making sure that it is not bending forward or back. Imagine you are standing between two panes of glass – this will protect your back.
3. Swing your right arm forward from your shoulder, straight out in front of you.
4. Swing the left arm simultaneously on the diagonal (i.e. while the right arm is forward the left arm is back).
5. Repeat on the left.
6. Repeat, leaning more and more to your side until you get a real feeling of falling. Let your head drop over to the side hanging over.
7. Let your other foot peel off the floor so you have a feeling of flying.

Tell the student to imagine they are throwing an old fashioned discus. Feel the weight, and visualise where they are throwing the discus to add a sense of direction.

☻ Lateral body swing (DVD: Exercise 17)

This swing needs release in the spine, pelvis and neck. It is the physicalisation of the 'swooning' feeling you have when someone you fancy enters the room.

Preparatory exercise for the lateral swing

1. Start in a squat position, knees wide apart and over the toes.
2. Come up through the spine in a primate position, arms loose and floppy.
3. Flop down.
4. Come up again a little higher this time and then flop down again.
5. Repeat four times until all the way up, then squat again.
6. Lift the bottom up and arch through again, this time lift and drop the spine and the using the thighs and the hands, push off the floor and lift and drop and lift and drop eight times or until there is a feeling of total release.
7. Return to standing and swing the arms across the body, releasing the knees when the arms fall.
8. Imagine someone is coming behind you and they touch you behind your knees and bottom of the back and then you flop down.
9. Repeat this eight times until you start finding the impulse and the release.
10. Go to the bottom with your head upside down and, to achieve the release, repeat the swing at the bottom of the swing (eight).
11. Then go upside down and to achieve the release, repeat the swing at the bottom of the swing and up.
12. Then from the upright position do release to the ground; to achieve the release, repeat the swing at the bottom of the swing and up.
13. Finally doing a grand swing and up.

Variations

- ○ Stand with the feet apart and look out onto the horizon.
- ○ Suddenly something is heard to the side.
- ○ Look over and sweep the arms up and out to the side.
- ○ You see your heart throb coming in the room.
- ○ You watch them walk towards you; when they are opposite you, you release and flop into the ground with a melting sigh.
- ○ Do the swing and come up.
- ○ By the time you are up your heart throb has carried on to the other side and you watch them go as you take your arms down to your side.

Teaching points

Make sure that the student's waist is lifted off their hips, and their legs are braced, with the spine lengthened and free. If the student's neck is poking forward of their pelvis pulled under, they will struggle to find release in this swing. Encourage the student to rediscover the sensation of the shoulder floating after they pressed against the wall (see p. 52–3).

⊚ The swing (DVD: Exercise 18)

1. Stand with the feet a little wider than the hips and take the arms out like wings.
2. Imagine somebody is touching you on the bottom of the spine and the back of the knees simultaneously.
3. Flop the body down and release the knees.
4. As the body reaches the bottom, the arms sweep forward and back across the front of the body at the same time as the legs are releasing.
5. There is a bound and rebound action resulting in the neck and head flopping and releasing. This then sends the student back to upright.

To achieve the release, repeat the swing at the bottom, resulting in 'Baby Lateral Body Swing'. Start with an arched back, the face looking up to the sky and the bottom floating out at the back, then do the swing and end up in the same position (**note**: make sure the neck and jaw are unlocked).

⊚ Full torso swing (DVD: Exercise 19)

This swing is probably the most dramatic of them all. It takes the student through physical space. It takes them to the highest possible place, without rising or distorting their body, and then drops with gravity, without falling down.

The swing has total release of the full torso and the fall gives momentum to return back up to a suspension, before settling like an autumn leaf to the ground. As with much of the movement, you need to have a free, strong released body to achieve the swing to its maximum level and to realise its full dramatic quality. The swing helps the body to become free, strong, released, suspended and working in space.

Preparation for the exercise

1. Stand with feet parallel and hang down through the spine.
2. Lift the torso slightly and drop. Lift and drop. Lift and drop, really making sure the head, neck and jaw are free.
3. Start taking this into a little heavy swing forward and back, brushing the ground with the hands, bouncing the knees on every drop.
4. Go to standing and take the arms up over the head.
5. Bend the knees and fall forward with the upper torso and when there is a feeling of free falling, release the knees and collapse, unlocking the jaw head and neck.
6. Do the lean forward, free fall with release into the swinging motion forward and back and forward and back, and release at the base of the swing. The head should carry on swinging on its own if it's being executed properly.
7. Repeat.
8. Free fall and swing back and forward, back and forward (at the base of the swing) and then swing the arms up to the suspended place.
9. Join it all up and do one free full torso swing.

The exercise

1. Stand with the feet hip width apart.
2. Draw the arms up the front parallel with each other.
3. Bend the knees slightly and bend forward from the waist, keeping the head in line with the arms.
4. When you feel as if you are about the fall forward into a free fall, release the knees further and drop the torso down, swinging the arms on the outside of the legs.
5. Have a feeling of bound and rebound, letting the back of the neck be free and loose, and the head heavy and the jaw released.
6. On the upward motion drive forward and out with the arms, keeping them by the ears.
7. Release into the knees.

Variations

○ Take a rise on to the toes as you are opening out your arms. Lower the heels at the same time as your arms lower by your side.
○ As you lower your arms and heels down from the 'rise' position, say a line of text and notice how the breath is free and the voice centred.
○ Perform it facing another person so that you are communicating in space.

☻ Fish net swing (DVD: Exercise 20)

1. Stand with feet hip width apart planted firmly onto the ground.
2. Lift the arms up, palms facing down.
3. Swing the body to the right spiralling round and down to the left, letting the arms wrap their way around the body and releasing the knees.

4. When the arms have completely released in their wrapped motion, throw them back out to the starting position but on a suspension as if you are casting a large fishing net over the sea.
5. Imagine you can see the horizon and let us see the sea in the eyes and sea spray on the face.
6. At the end of the suspension, spiral the body round to the left, wrapping the arms around the body on the outward breath.
7. Repeat several times as required.

Encourage the student to imagine that they are a fisherman casting a large net over a vast sea.

⊙ Leg swings (DVD: Exercise 21)

Leg swings help the actor to walk in a free and open way. Obviously all characters do not have the same walk, but this is for the universal walk which then can be tailored to the needs of each character. If the actor only has a tight, locked walk, this could restrict their physical acting choices and possibilities to transform into different characters.

1. Stand with the feet parallel and the left hand holding onto a ballet barre, wall bars, the wall or a partner's shoulder for balance. While the partner is standing there, it is a good opportunity for them to practice their natural stance, as the same time as giving balance to the swinging partner.
2. Keeping the body as neutral as possible, pick up the right knee with the right hand and pull it tight into the right shoulder, or as near as possible, without distorting the torso, keeping the ankle and foot dangling.
3. Drop the leg heavily to the floor.
4. Using the right hand, take hold of the right ankle, lifing the foot to the buttock, whilst keeping the left leg braced. Make sure that both knees are together and the hips down. Using the impetus from the pelvic rock, drop the leg to the floor and swish it forward, ensuring that the feet and knees are parallel an arc swing with the leg.
5. When the suspension of the swing at the front of the body is complete, drop the right leg to the floor, swishing it behind you, again keeping the feet and knees parallel. (For the reader who has done ballet, this movement is similar to that of battement en cloches, without the turn out and the tension!)
6. Repeat forward and back, making sure there is a heavy drop in the centre. Be careful not to stub the toe on the floor; lift off the supporting hip whilst swinging and this should help.

Repeat steps 1–5 on the left leg (alternating with the post so you take it in turns to stand still, and practise your stance in an active way). After practising leg swings holding on for balance, stand in the centre of the room and repeat the exercise with no prop or partner. If the students find it hard to balance, then a technique that can be used is to hold on to the opposite ear to balance or use the imagery of you holding onto the balance strap in an Underground train.

Last and most importantly, finish the exercise by walking around the room to feel how the leg swing has improved the walk.

> **Teaching point**
>
> *This swing should be activated from the pelvis. If the student can keep the pelvis lifter out of the supporting hip, they will avoid crashing their foot down on the floor and causing potential injury. As the student is swinging their legs, tell them to imagine that they are walking along the road, or running along a beach.*

Figure of eight leg swing

This is an advanced swing and needs a loose free hip and knee joint. It takes a lot of balance and flexibility. It is normally done in the second year of training.

1. Stand holding onto a partner's shoulder, barre or wall as in the regular leg swing.
2. Put your right hand on your hip and extend the right leg out to the back, diagonally right.
3. Draw a figure of eight on the floor, turning in your foot. Feel the weight in the leg as it crosses in front of you, then turn it out on the top curve, keep it turned out at the neck of the eight and keep it turned out at the back left diagonal and start turning it in on the back loop.
4. Turn around and do this on the left leg.
5. Then turn back onto the right side and lift it off at the back and then swing the same pattern that you have drawn on the floor, making sure you apply that same technique.

Variation

○ When you have achieved this add the arm in a complementary figure of eight swing.
○ Try this in the centre without holding on.
○ Try mixing the swings, for example, four straight, four figure of eight, four straight, four figure of eight.

☻ **Swings travelling** (DVD: Exercise 22)

It is important that after the student has learnt the swings within their own body, they can also use the swing to get from one point to another. In movement terms, this is referred to as 'travelling'; that is, moving across the space from one point to another, through actions such as running, skipping, galloping, leaping and hopping.

When swinging across the space at a gallop, the student must use their feet, calves and thighs to allow the arms, face, neck and jaw to be released and free. The feeling of travelling through space with the momentum of a swing is, at first, like being on a roller-coaster. It is important for the student not only to be able to move on their own but also for them to be able to relate to others. It is also important to begin using the voice with the body as early as possible so that the two are integrated.

Here are some examples of swings travelling across the room.

Bow and arrow travelling
See bow and arrow swings, p. 54, for further description.

1. Stand opposite a partner in the top left-hand corner of the room.
2. Close your arms together, pulling the bow back and dropping the front arm.
3. Swing the arm forward and back, forward and back, while remaining on the spot.
4. Gallop across the room, down towards the bottom right-hand corner, swinging the back arm over and over. This swing can also be done galloping backwards.

The image of the golden cloak helps the student to use their body in a dramatic, and not a purely functional, way. You can encourage each actor student to see their partner as a 'scene partner', and thus to communicate to each other through their movement.

Variations
○ You can alternate each swing with a complete circular journey of the arm.
○ Keep the body strong and centred allowing only the arm to have a free flowing movement.
○ Transfer the weight between each swing.
○ Release the head and sternum on each swing allowing your body to bend forward from the chest area, not the waist (as that could possibly hurt the back).

When the students have mastered the movement with plenty of release and freedom, add the voice, i.e. 'One and two and three and four', or 'One and two and three and four and hey and hey and hey and hey'.

Swinging both arms over, bending down and peeping through
1. Face your partner, take both arms above your head and lean top right diagonal.
2. Swing under and back and under and back (really looking at your partner), using your upper torso, but go no lower than the waist.
3. Swing both arms over and over, keeping the body upright at this point, then bend over towards the bottom left-hand corner, peeping through on the second count of 'and one' as you are galloping, really using your thighs, ankles and feet to propel you down the diagonal.

Variations
○ As in exercise 1, use a supported sound.

Figure of eight arm swing
See figure of eight swing (p. 55) for further description.

1. Stand opposite a partner at the top right-hand corner of the room.
2. Left the arm nearest the corner, as if taking up a golden cloak.
3. Do four figure of eight arm swings, standing on the spot.

4. Swing the same arm over and over four times whilst galloping on the diagonal towards the bottom left-hand corner.
5. Stand still on the swing and repeat four figure of eight arm swings.
6. Repeat galloping and swinging the arm over and over.

Note: keep your torso aligned whilst you are swinging over and over.

Teaching tips

The image of the golden cloak can be used to help the student to use their body in a dramatic, not purely functional way. You can encourage each student to see their partner as a 'scene partner' and thus to communicate to each other through their movement.

When swinging across the floor in twos, it is important for the teacher to keep the flow of the class moving by making sure the students are ready for their turn.

Forearm and backhand swing

1. Stand on two feet facing you partner.
2. Float your arm up, thinking of your golden cloak.
3. Gallop and swing simultaneously over and over and then turn back to back and repeat the movements, but 'backhanded', as in the tennis stroke. So the swing goes: forehand, backhand, forehand, backhand.
4. Keep galloping and turning back on yourself as you swing.

To keep the class going, the first couple start with the forehand swing; when they turn back to back, the next couple start with the forehand swing. As the pairs move across the room, alternate pairs will be facing in and out.

Two armed partner swing in space

This next swing is still on the diagonal, with half the group starting at the bottom left hand corner of the room and the other half at the top right hand corner.

1. To the constant roll of the drum the first pair run toward each other, arms out stretched.
2. As soon as they meet they clasp forearms and lean back, really falling back and trusting each other. They then run, feet side to side , their toes together (running sideways).
3. Next they swing round and round like a wheel, with their toes in the centre and their bodies leaning out.

The teacher should use a drum to create a rhythm – keeping an element of control to the movement. You can also bang the drum when the movement seems to be getting out of control. This swing should give the appearance of being 'out-of-control', but the students should be safe and able to stop when asked. Like with many scenes, the wildness is underpinned by technique.

Preparation

1. Stand opposite a partner and hold hands (or forearms if your hands are slippery). If you have a tall and short person or two people with very differing weights, then try and balance this out with experimentation.
   - ○ The taller or heavier person will be more erect whilst the shorter or lighter person will have their feet nearer the other person and their stance will be lower back.
   - ○ Lean back, pulling away from one another, taking each other's weight.
2. Stretch the arms fully.
3. Repeat with everybody in the class.

Extra exercises for precision and suspension

Run and fly (for balance)

1. Run in the space and then stop on one leg.
2. Lift the other leg behind you, with your arms out like wings.
3. Hover and fly, looking out over a cliff edge.

☻ Je prend (DVD: Exercise 23)

1. Stand in neutral with the feet a little wider than the hips.
2. Look to the right.
3. Move the right foot out to the side.
4. Take an imaginary object with the right hand and bring the left leg to join the right leg, hip-width apart, parallel bringing the body up to the imaginary object.
6. Look to the left.
7. Move the left foot out to the left, keeping the right hand where it is.
8. Take an object with left hand.
9. Look back and discard the object in the right hand.
10. Move up to the new object.

☻ Contre tension (DVD: Exercise 24)

1. Stand with the legs wider than the hips, and bend the knees and extend the arms away from the body.
2. Look to the left.
3. Move the body over to the left knee, keeping the right leg extended, to where the head is looking.
4. Turn the body over the left bent knee.
5. Look to the right.
6. Move the body in the direction of where the head is looking, ending up with the right knee bent and the left leg extended.
7. Turn the body over the right leg.
8. Repeat with many different breath patterns, as this changes the drama of the movement.

6 Dynamic movement: The Cat

The Cat is a series of movements that have been adapted from a Grotowski concept of movement. The Cat pushes the student to the physical extreme and abilities and therefore provokes responses from the whole person. Each action induces a flow of thought, feeling and sensation, and often impacts on deep memories which feeds the dynamic momentum of the experience.

Eventually, The Cat will be performed as a whole sequence, with each movement linking seamlessly to the next. However, at first it is important to break down every single movement; once each stage is mastered, they can be put together into one long movement sequence which allows a dynamic flow of thought. At its best, The Cat can seem like a piece of theatre in itself.

⊙ **Teaching points** (DVD: Exercise 25)

The movements in The Cat are to be executed at the student's own level. It is not a competition to see who is the strongest or the most supple. The movements improve the student's strength and suppleness; the purpose of the exercise is to improve every aspect of the student's physicality.

The exercise can be used in several ways. Firstly, as a warm-up for the body, as well as a very good overall fitness routine. The repetition allows the student to build on their technique and allows the exercise to become an active meditation, and ultimately leads to the students being able to use the exercise before rehearsal and performance as their own, personal warm-up.

Secondly, it can be a warm up which incorporates the drama of the play. It could warm-up the whole company and it could have a theme running through it which is the setting of the world of the play.

Thirdly, it can be done opposite a partner, ideally the person you are acting with. You could, for example, explore one person being high status and the other of low status, or both in love, or one person interested and the other's interest elsewhere. The dramatic possibilities are countless.

Fourthly, it can be done as you are running the text with your scene partner. It would be an

---

ideal warm up to do it once through with a vocal warm up, and then again, using the text of the play.

Fifthly, it can be practised in a small space so it would be possible to do some of it in your dressing room or trailer on a film set. There is no excuse not to keep the body warmed up and flexible in tandem with the voice.

Without exception, the actors say it is easier to practise it using a dramatic image, as it alleviates from the strain some people feel when executing the movements for the first time.

The first ten movements are by far the easiest in which to achieve a dramatic thought, because the movements are more feline; after that it can be harder as the movements are less feline and more gymnastic.

The Cat – sequence of movements

Imagine you are a kitten, waking up after a nap and needing food. You find a bowl of milk. Imagine you are a great big cat waking up and the food is raw meat. Either way, you will experience changes in the physicality and quality of the way you execute the exercise.

Start by lying on your tummy totally floppy and relaxed, with the arms down by the sides of the body, head on one side, facing the left (Photos to show each posture) 30 in all

Yawn and stretch

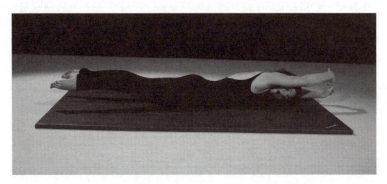

This is a full yawn and which stretches through the body, like a baby or a cat waking up. The stretch is full and luxurious and is very good to get the body prepared before going into quite strenuous movement.

1. Start by yawning and stretching all the way through the body, wriggling through the spine, ribs and then all the way through to the extremities keeping the fingers and toes in contact with the floor.
2. Relax back down to the floor with the head to the right, as if going back to sleep. Repeat the stretch on the other side, head to the left.

Head lift

This is a stretch of the neck, still in 'sleeping' mode.

1. Imagining you are a cat, wake up and sleepily look around you, lifting only the head.
2. Then place the head back down facing the right, and totally relax as if going back to sleep.
3. Repeat, placing your head down to the other side.

Teaching point

Make sure the student's jaw is unlocked and their face is soft.

Demi-cobra

1. Lift the whole body up, keeping the legs and feet in contact with the floor and looking around as if searching for food, then lower the body and allow the body to relax, head to the right, keeping the feet in contact with the floor and the arms down by your side.
2. Repeat the demi-cobra, building the hungry for food image, and lower the body and head to the left.

Teaching point

Make sure that the student's body is lifted up as high as possible; they shouldn't push further than the capabilities of their body.

Full cobra

1. Lift the upper body off the floor (really concentrating on your food or prey) then add the hands, in line with the shoulders, elbows close to the body and then push the body up, keeping the head in line with the spine, bottom soft and hips dropping into the floor.

Teaching point

If the student has a stiff back then put the hands further forward in front of their body.

Jack knife

1. Tuck your toes under, lift your bottom to the plank position, then send the bottom right back and stretch the body and head under the arms; stretch the heels towards the ground (in yoga this position is normally referred to as downward dog).

> **Teaching point**
> *Most of the time in movement training for the actor, the tummy must have released muscles in order not to tighten and lock the breath for the speaking voice. However, if there are some exercises which need to support the back, then the tummy needs to be pulled up and the bottom held tightly to prevent injury to the back. This also builds strength in the tummy which is needed for health and fitness Be aware that, to protect the back in the plank position, the tummy needs to be pulled in. The tummy must be released afterwards.*

Hip roll

This is done quickly with an outward breath. The pelvis drops and swings round. It is not performed slowly as it can be too strenuous on the spine.

1. Drop the right hip to the floor (without touching), roll the pelvis towards the floor, roll so left hip is towards the floor.
2. Then send the hips back and up, looking under the arms in the jack knife position.
3. Repeat to the left.

> **Teaching point**
> *The arms need to remain straight, otherwise the movement turns into a press-up. To break down this movement, advise the students to get onto their hands and knees and circle their spines, making sure the head is involved and the jaw free.*

Leg kick

This is an extreme movement which incorporates qualities from ballet, gymnastics and martial arts. The shape of the leg and foot when the knee is drawn into the nose, as well as the swing of the leg round and up, is reminiscent of a round house kick, and the position where the leg is up in the air is like a cross between a large balletic arabesque and the post in acrobatics.

1. Get into the plank position and at the same time draw the right knee up to your nose, leg turned right out and have a flexed foot (see foot positions, pp. 29–30), pelvis dropped to the floor.
2. Kick the right leg out towards the nose, arms kept straight, then swing the right leg out and up into a high lift using the hands for support. Gently lower the foot to the floor to resume the jack knife position.

Teaching point

Work firstly on all fours (this is perhaps the best option if students find the exercise strenuous). Secondly, repeat with the pelvis touching the ground, this enables the leg kick to be lined up, but be very careful as it is very demanding on the groin and back. Thirdly, repeat the exercise in the plank position, as above.

Indian push through

This movement is very similar to a press-up except it is not only building strength in the upper body and arms, it is also supplying and stretching the muscles at the same time, thus encouraging stretched flexible muscle instead of just bulk, which as mentioned before, can tighten the breath and chest and lead to injury.

1. Make sure the palms are flat to the ground, with fingers spread, fingertips alongside the chest. Elbows should be tight to the sides. Press down through the top of the feet, pressing all ten toes into the floor. The only parts of the body touching the floor should be the tops of the feet and the hands. This prevents too much pressure on the lower back. From the jack knife position, look up and bending the elbows in a smooth transient movement, scoop the chest down towards the floor, followed by the tummy, then pelvis and thighs, to end up in the upward dog position.

2. When you are in full cobra, reverse the movement by bending the elbows, so that the tail bone lifts up as the body, chest and head end up back in the jack knife position. Sometimes floating the elbows out is easier if the press up is hard to accomplish. Sometimes keeping the elbows tucked in works better for the body. Whichever way, the exercise builds up strength in the arms and uses different muscle groups.

Teaching point

Students can begin by practising the Indian push through on their hands and knees. They should try to connect each part of the body with the floor one by one, starting with the chest, then the tummy, then the thighs (arching the spine into the cobra position). When the movement is executed like this in the physical memory, do it on the hands and feet.

Pounce and pike

Again this is easier and more dramatic if it is done with a dramatic image and without holding the poses for too long.

1. Start from the jack knife and pull the hips back, twisting the knees to the right whilst trying to leave the arms where they are and looking forward as if you are going to pounce upon the food.

2. Indian push through (see Indian push through above) from the pounced position.

Teaching point

The arms will stretch out here and the right arm will contract and even leave the floor.

Folded leaf

1. Let the whole body fold into the floor over bent knees, the head on the ground and the arms outstretched like the prayer position or Child's pose in yoga.

The three back arches

1. From the folded leaf, uncurl through the spine, taking the arms above the head as you rise onto your toes.
2. Open the arms as if saluting the gods or the sun, and look up to the sky (the sun reflecting on your face).
3. Return the upper body to its central position by lifting the arms up over the head, again squeezing your buttocks to protect your spine and arch your body back down to a folded leaf position.
   - ○ Slip the knees open.
   - ○ Uncurl up through the spine, taking the arms over the head and opening the body to the sun, as before, then open the arms a fraction further to touch the ankles, pushing the pelvis forward.

Teaching point

*It will help the student to squeeze the buttocks at this point which will protect the back. They **must not** crunch the neck back, but keep it in alignment and open the jaw to prevent putting strain in the neck and throat.*

Headstand

Preparation

1. Place the hands and head so they make a triangle on the floor (head in front of the hands).
2. Place the part of the head between the crown and the forehead on the floor. If you set your head too much into the crown, then the body will go into a forward roll. If you set it too much into your forehead the legs will never get up above your head. Pull the legs straight up, toes on the floor. Tuck in the tummy using core strength to lift the legs above the head.
3. Balance with the knees kept close into the body for control.
4. When balanced in this position, arch the back a little until the centre of gravity has changed and the bottom is further over the head. Very carefully take the legs up. Use the hands and the muscles in the back and bottom to balance and then lift all the way up. Get someone to check that the body is straight.
5. Keep practising this on its own until the student can manage it smoothly and then finally when it's possible, practise making the headstand one continuous, flowing movement ending with a balance.

If the student cannot manage it introduce the balance on the hands (instead of the head) in the big squat position (see below).

Big squat balance

1. Stand with the legs wide apart.
2. Lift the arms up over the head and put the hands together in a prayer position, on a breath in.
3. Breathe out at the same time as bending the knees until the student is in a squatting position.
4. Place the elbows inside the thighs and press the knees out over the toes, keeping the heels on the floor.
5. Open the palms of the hands to face the front.

To balance

○ Fall onto the hands, pressing the knees out with the elbows.
○ Fall back on to the feet, and then back on to the hands.
○ Balance.

Teaching points

To build the strength for a headstand, the student should place their forearms on the floor and place the body in a jack knife position on their elbows. They should then move their body forward and back as if looking for something over the hands and under the hands. This exercise builds strength in the shoulders, and core, building the right sort of strength for the headstand.

Big back arch to the floor

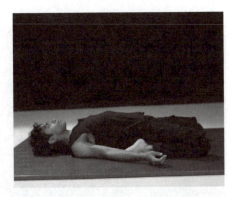

1. Come back down to the folded leaf and slip the knees open wide.
2. Uncurl through the spine all the way up and then arch backwards until the head touches the floor.
3. Slide down, vertebra by vertebra, until the back is fully in contact with the floor. Once in this position, stay there.

This is a lovely stretch for the front of the thighs and will help to open the pelvis and release the voice.

Teaching points

If you have bad knees, bad back or ankles and the exercise is painful, kneel with the legs spread and ease the bottom to the ground. Only when it is comfortable enough to place the bottom on the ground, consider going back into the floor.

Using the backs of the hands as stabilisers and really open them out like wings. If the student feels stiff then let them just go down as far as they can before melting the body into the floor.

Flipping out your legs

1. Lift your pelvis up and wriggle your feet out from underneath you and lie on your back with the knees on the chest and the feet relaxed on the bottom.
2. Bounce your feet on your bottom like a baby.
3. Bounce your feet three times on your bottom and then stretch your legs straight up pointing your toes and then flop them back down and repeat three times, making sure you bottom stays in contact with the floor.

Three bridges

1. Place the feet on the floor next to the bottom, semi-supine, and this time keep the feet together.
2. Keep the arms by the sides as the student pushes up through the spine, vertebrae by vertebrae, until they reach the neck.
3. Roll back down through spine to the bottom again.
4. Lift and open the legs until they are a hip width apart in semi-supine and the arms are out to the side.
5. Push up through the spine and back up to the neck and then return vertebrae by vertebrae, back to the floor.
6. Lift and open the legs so they are just wider than the hips and then push up through the spine, arms outstretched above the head flat and on the floor. Add the hands, by the ears and then push up into a big bridge, stretching into the shoulders. Care needs to be taken because although when you are a small child it is absolutely fine to push up into a bridge, when you are an adult, especially if you are an adult male, it is a difficult movement to achieve; it is far easier, and better for your body, to push up into your shoulders to avoid injuring the base of your spine.
7. Uncurl through the spine back to the floor.
8. Swing the legs over the head, so the legs are straight and together and the toes are pointed on the floor (sometimes called the plough position), while holding onto the back with your hands and squeezing the elbows towards each other.

The three scissors

1. In the plough position, keep the legs straight with the toes pointed onto the floor over the head.
2. Open them very wide with the feet on the floor and then snap them together, pointing the toes.
3. Lift the feet about 70cms (2ft) off the floor..
4. Keep the legs in the same position and then open them wide.
5. Then snap them together.
6. Lift the feet another 70cms (2ft) into the air and then snap them together.
7. Repeat one more time until the legs, pelvis and torso are all in line with each other in a full shoulder-stand, squeezing the elbows together for support.

Three leg twists

1. From the very high shoulder-stand, turn the knees down to the right shoulder, in a twisting motion and then stretch them right back up again to the high shoulder-stand.
2. Turn the knees to the left shoulder, and then back up again.
3. Turn the knees back to the right shoulder and open out the arms and then place the knees over the shoulder onto the floor behind (shoulder roll).

Yoga headstand

1. Draw a triangle on the ground in front of you and then interlink the your fingers and place the elbows and forearms on the floor, on either side of the triangle.
2. Place your head in your hands on the top point of the triangle.
3. Tuck your knees into your chest and lift up onto your head and elbows and explore the balance.
4. Arch your back so your bottom goes over your head and then stretch your legs up to the ceiling.
5. Come back down onto your knees and open the arms out wide.

The following combination is performed first on one leg then the other.

Forward shoulder roll

1. Forward shoulder roll over your right shoulder (tucking your head under your left arm, all the way over until you are sitting on your bottom with your right knee bent up to the ceiling and the left leg stretched out in front of you).

Backward shoulder roll

1. From the sitting position with your left leg outstretched and your right knee bent roll backwards taking your right leg over your right shoulder, and keeping your arms stretched out in front.

2. End the roll on your knee in a long lunge, on your right knee, with the left leg stretched out behind you.

Three salutations to the sun on the right

1. From the long lunge position, with the body lying over the bent leg, uncurl through your spine and take your arms above your head (even though you are over the bent leg and the other one is stretched out behind, try to feel as if you are standing on two feet and then it will help you with your posture).

2. Open your arms wide, while making sure they are connected between your shoulder blades like wings.

3. Look up to the sky, feeling the sun reflecting on your face, and again (as in the back arches) make sure you are not restricting the air flow in your neck or throat.

4. After bringing your arms over your head, fold back down to the floor.
5. Repeat this three times, feeling the body open and create any image – face to the sun, rain drops on your face – anything that helps you feel open and free.

Three sweeping the sky on the right

1. Turn to face the side with the right leg still bent and the left leg outstretched and with the knee facing the ceiling.
2. Sweep the right arm out and up, stretch through the rib cage and sweep the arm through to the finger tips, sweeping the sky and then bend over the outstretched leg on your side, placing the left hand on the left leg outstretched as near to the foot as you can manage.
3. Fold the body down over the left leg.
4. Fold back on your side and then sweep the back of your hand up over the sky again, and back down by your side. This is usually done on the count of three i.e. up 2, 3 over 2, 3 down 2, 3 on your side 2, 3 and back down 2, 3).
5. Repeat the movement three times.

Note: the more you stretch, the more flexible your body will become. The more flexible your body is the greater flexibility you will have in your physicality and character choices.

Swastika on the right leg

1. Swing the left leg behind you and if you are very free in your hips then make a swastika shape with your legs. If you are not so free then close the legs towards the body. Flexibility of the position will come with practice. Place the left hand on the right ankle and the right hand on the floor next to your right knee. This shape is a swastika (Hindu peace sign).
2. Fold the body forward over the leg, arching through the spine until finally the head touches on the floor in front of you.
3. Uncurl up through the spine until you are sitting on both sitting bones (i.e. the base of the pelvis).
4. Sink into the back leg, opening the hip further and then roll up to lengthen the spine.
5. Repeat three times and then swing the left or back leg over into a yoga spinal twist.

Yoga spinal twist

This is a deep spiral twist for the spine and internal organs and this position offers a very dramatic pose and form of a wringing movement.

1. Lift your left leg over your right, placing the foot against the outside of the right knee. Bring your right heel in close to your buttocks. Keep the spine erect.
2. Stretch your arms out to the sides at shoulder level and twist around to the left.
3. Bring the right arm down on the outside of the left knee and hold your left foot with your right hand, placing your left hand on the floor behind you. As you exhale, twist as far as possible to the left. Look over the left shoulder.
4. Walk three steps forward, reach as if to touch something and then recoil, into a backward shoulder roll.

Backward shoulder roll

This supports a dramatic moment and if you were doing The Cat with a partner this would be a moment of connection with the person, and the touch could take the form of a fight, a caress etc. The backward shoulder roll ends up with you on one knee in a long lunge position over the left leg.

1. Uncurl from the yoga spinal twist and press onto the front foot, using the muscles in the left thigh while lengthening the spine up and forward. You don't need to use your hands.
2. Walk forward right leg, left leg, right leg and then reach to touch something with your left arm, your left leg is stretched behind, pulling in the opposite direction to recoil the body. Leaning forward to sit down with the left leg bent and the right leg outstretched, roll back over the left shoulder looking to the left and ending up on your left knee, body folded over it and arms outstretched in front in a Swan Lake position.

Three salutations to the sun on the left

1. From the long lunge position, with the body lying over the bent leg, uncurl through the spine and take your arms above your head (even though you are over the bent leg and the other one is stretched out behind, try to feel as if you are standing on two feet and then it will help your posture).

2. Open your arms wide while making sure they are connected between your shoulder blades like wings.
3. Look up to the sky, feeling the sun reflecting on your face, and again (as in the back arches) make sure you are not restricting the air flow in your neck and throat.
4. After bringing your arms over your head, fold back down to the floor.
5. Repeat three times, feeling the body open and create any image – face to the sun, rain drops on your face – anything that helps you fell open and free.

Three sweeping the sky stretches on the left

1. Turn to face the side with the left leg still bent and the right leg outstretched and with the knees facing the ceiling.
2. Sweep the left arm out and up, stretch through the rib cage and sweep the arm through to the fingers, sweeping the sky and then bend over the outstretched leg on your side, placing the right hand on the right leg, outstretched as near to the foot as you can manage.
3. Fold the body down over the right leg.
4. Fold back on your side and sweep the back of your hand up over the sky again, and back down by your side. This is usually done on the count of three, i.e. up, 2, 3; over, 2, 3; down, 2, 3; on your side, 2, 3; and back down, 2, 3.
5. Repeat the movement three times.

Swastika on the left leg

1. Swing the right leg behind you and if you are very free in your hips then make a swastika shape with your legs. If you are not so free then close the legs towards the body. Flexibility of the position will come with practice. Place the right hand on the left ankle and the left hand on the floor next to your left knee. This shape is a swastika (Hindu peace sign).
2. Fold the body forward over the leg, arching through the spine until finally the head touches the floor in front of you.
3. Uncurl up through the spine until you are sitting on both sitting bones (i.e. the base of the pelvis).
4. Sink into the back leg, opening the hip further and then roll up to lengthen the spine.
5. Repeat three times and then swing the right, or back, leg over into a yoga spinal twist.

Three recurring shoulder rolls over the right and left shoulders

1. Stand on the right leg, using your right thigh muscles, pushing off the left, or back, foot and lengthening through the spine and out of the top of your head.
2. Walk forward left, right, left, stretching the right arm forward and the right foot behind.
3. Touch something and recoil over the right shoulder onto the right knee.
4. Swing the left leg round and stand up on it and walk forward right, left, right.
5. Touch something with the left hand and backward shoulder roll over the left shoulder on to the left knee.
6. Repeat on the right again and then walk forward as if to repeat and then stop with feet parallel and full torso swing (see p. 59).
7. Rise on your toes and lower back down again, bring your arms down by your sides.

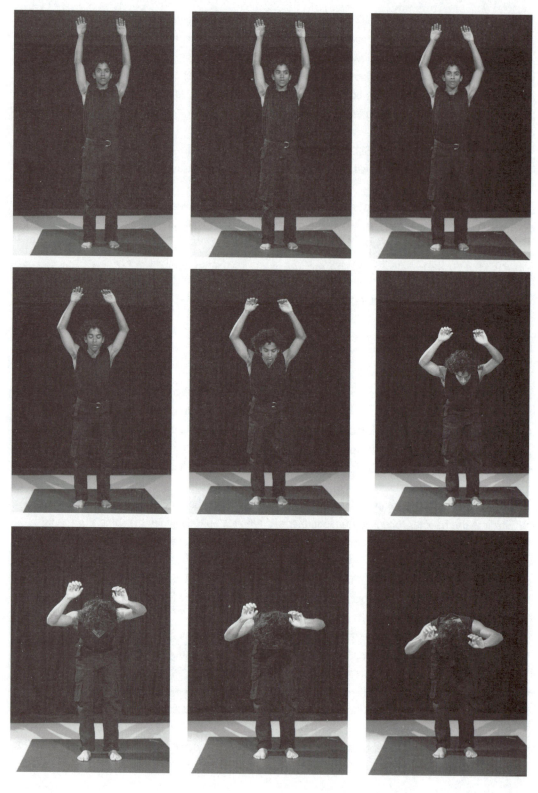

Conclusion

At the end of The Cat the student will feel fully stretched, strong, free and released. The body and imagination will be warmed up, as will the breath for the voice. The student will feel exhilarated, and ready to transform into character for rehearsal or performance.

7 Acrobatics and tumbling for the acting student

If there is a play which requires an acrobat, then often the casting director will approach a circus school or use a gymnast with an Equity card to fit the bill.

What the actor can contribute is different to what a dancer or gymnast can contribute. The actor can use expression and imagination through what can be plastic movement. Plastic movement is the term used for movement which is physical and muscular but which is executed without thought and imagination.

For the training of the actor, acrobatics is used for bravery, balance, control, suppleness, strength and partner work, and transferable skills, such as trust, listening and receiving. This is achieved by the students experiencing the physical action of one student lifting or catching another, whilst that first student is using their body in a potentially dangerous way. Students learn that in gymnastics and acrobatics, physical and emotional trust and non-verbal communication is vital for health and safety, in acting the same qualities are needed for them to feel safe on the stage with one another. If a student experiences the physical sensation of danger or achievement when performing a trick which they have found difficult to master, then when they are in a challenging acting situation, they can remember that sensation, which can then translate into an emotionally brave piece of work. Acrobatics can also be used in a dramatic context using the skills to fulfil the dramatic image of the director, for example, if the director is using a cast of actors to illustrate the text in a physical manner, then acrobatic skills can be used to create mountains, rivers, caterpillars, monsters, trees, caves and animals.

From the start, it is important that there is no segregation or streaming of the students. It is important to keep the class together and to create the appropriate atmosphere for ensemble work. It is also most important for every student to feel that they have an importance within the class and that the work develops at the unique pace of each individual student. It is not about who is naturally best, but who can break through the furthest in transferable skills.

Pure acrobatics

Pure movement is used as a basis for everything else in movement training. It is wise to think of the acrobatics as pure movement, which has advanced on to more complex body movement, that way any student who has had a bad experience of gymnastic classes, will be able to think in terms of acting through the movement, rather than failing at a skill.

An example of an acrobatic class for actors

Divide the class up into three groups.

1. **General warm-up**

   This can include very physical games such as Cat and Mouse, Ships and Shores or the Music Game (see Chapter 1).

2. **Warm-up for specific parts of the body**

   Then take the warm up into more specific parts of the body. For example, some rib stretches, shake downs, arm, leg and body swings, followed by The Cat.

3. **Acrobatics**

   ○ All types of rolls – forward, backward; side into high jumps, star jumps, tuck jumps, and turning jumps; into straddles and falls.

   ○ Cartwheels – these should be done firstly facing the right side of the room, followed by the left side using two hands. The exercise can then be extended by using one hand only, firstly on the right hand and then the left, facing the right side of the room and repeated facing the left. A further extension would be to link some of the movements together, for example, cartwheels into side rolls into cartwheels .

   ○ Handstands – handstands into forward rolls; handstands into bridges; backward rolls to hand stands.

   ○ Arab springs.

   ○ Hand springs.

   ○ Back flips.

   ○ No-handed cartwheels.

   ○ Somersaults.

Health and safety

I will not attempt to teach the above on the page, as it could be dangerous for the reader to attempt these tricks without proper instructions. They are a guide to what most adults can achieve with proper instruction.

Partner work

There are many acrobatic tricks that can be done with a partner. This builds trust between the actors.

Teaching points

The pair should have good communication, which is clear, decisive and non-emotional. They must also listen to each other and react accordingly (just like acting). This is not the moment for joking, pranks or mistrust. For example, if one person tells the other to get off, then that person must do so straight away. They must never in this situation prevaricate as they can't see the other person properly. Always do as you are asked and then discuss what went wrong and then start again.

The above teaching points refer to all of the following:

Back lifts

Stand back to back. A lifts B up and over their shoulders. A must lift B by their arm pits and not their arms. They must lift B's body up and out of their spine and lean forwards, bending their knees and then finally placing their elbows on to their knees for safety. After repeating several times, this can be extended: A gradually bends down to the ground, slipping the hips out from under them and extending their legs out until they are lying flat on the front of their body. B, meanwhile, relaxes the entire time, ending up lying on their back on top of A's back, trusting A.

Variation 1

After A has stretched B in the manner of a back lift, A then places B's hands to the floor and eases B over their A while simultaneously B squeezes the bottom and opens the legs like a backward walk over. It is very important to get the positioning of the bodies and legs right otherwise the spine can be crushed or the arms can collapse. Proper positioning of the bodies allows for an easy transition.

Variation 2

A puts one foot in front of the other and places their hands on to the ground while B does a handstand up A's arms and back until their bottoms meet. A bends the knees and then lifts B up to the feet making an easy forward walk over.

Sitting on shoulders

This can be done by A bending down and B simply sitting on A's shoulders. More elaborately, A stands still and B goes behind them. B then makes a handstand up A's back and A takes B's ankles and pulls him off his arms. B stays relaxed as he is lifted off the ground. A bends forward until their back is parallel to the floor and then as they stand up B sits up simultaneously and shifts their crotch into A's neck and hooks their feet round A's back, placing their hands on A's forehead.

Standing on shoulders

A stands on two feet with their legs apart. B faces A and holds both A's hands. The right one in A's right hand and the left in A's left hand. B puts their left foot into A's thigh and then swings the right foot onto the right shoulder and then, with A pulling the arms, B swings the left foot onto the left shoulder. A holds on to B's right ankle with their right hand and left ankle with their left hand and keeping the knees bent and the toes hanging over the shoulders and their weight forward, they then stand up.

Standing on backs

One person is on all fours; the other person stands on their back. The person on top must have one foot between the shoulder blades and the other foot at the bottom of the back and turned out. The person on top has to work quickly and efficiently and without fear. If they go up slowly, heavily and with fear of either falling off or of hurting the other person, then it will hurt the other person. If, on the other hand, they go up quickly and efficiently then the person underneath will hardly feel them.

Chest stands

One person is on all fours and the other hooks their arms under their torso. They then kick up into a chest stand (a no-handed handstand). Use the other person for balance and control.

Flying angel

One person lies on the floor with their arms and legs in the air. The other person places their hands on the other person's hands and their hips on the other person's feet. The person underneath bends their knees and when they stretch them the other person flies up into the air like a flying angel or superman; they need to lift their body and legs up into the air while at the same time, squeezing their bottom.

8 Neutral mask

Mask work is divided into two main categories: neutral mask and character mask. Although mask work can be a means in itself, for actor training purposes the mask is used as a tool to allow the body to speak and to be expressive.

For the purposes of the universal body, this chapter will look at the neutral mask. Character mask will be looked at here to show how the neutral body can go into transformation.

Greek tragedies work on a heroic scale and require the actor to play larger than life, appropriate to the themes of the great plays. In this respect, any experience with mask training will be of value. Masks can teach the student to be economical, bold and comfortable, whilst moving. Each movement is precise and simple, done with total commitment. When the face is hidden and the voice is quiet, the actor needs to communicate through their body and its movements. When the movements are simple and economical, a mask seems to invest the space around it with its presence. The presence is the energy and life force the mask brings to the room. It charges the surrounding air with importance. The entire face and body must be regarded as a unit. The mask requires a tempo different to that of daily life and is highly effective in stillness. The actor must refrain from preconceived ideas; they must not tell the mask what to do, but listen to it.

As with high, low, wide, narrow, the diagonals and the twenty movement work, there is a form to the mask. The exercises are set up by the teacher, along with the rules, but the creativity, timing, breath and drama come from the student or actor.

The movement must not be plastic like a dancer or gymnast, but filled with thought and emotion which must come before the reaction. That is, the thought and feeling must come before the action. The natural movements need to be enlarged to correspond with the mask and must be slow and clear of any fussiness. The student must sustain the focus and make definite movement choices, for example when they need to stop, be very clear. There should be no symbolism or explanatory gesture. The movement comes from the precision of observation and sense of memory.

Because the mask eliminates the actor's face and its mobility, two of their main resources, they force the actor to communicate through their body. The neutral mask takes the actor away from the personal. It makes everything larger and more important, in the sense that one cannot be man, but mankind.

Because some of the mask work is clearly from Jacques LeCoq, Trish Arnold's notes have been incorporated from LeCoq's teaching.

When using or working with a mask, it must be clear that it:

1. Is not an intellectual essay.
2. It is not symbolism.
3. It is not a special technical invention.

It is the translation by the body of personalities, sensations and feelings extracted by the dramatic situation to lean towards great clarity and truthfulness.

Discarding all extremes of interfering gestures, the student will go:

1. From the concrete to the abstract.
2. From observation to imagination.
3. From particular to general.
4. From simple to complicated.

According to Le Coq, the student should not attempt moral themes (Seven Deadly Sins; pride, avarice etc.) until they have mastered physical realities (drunkenness, age, fat, hunger).

The mask will laugh, be afraid, look, be the face of an old man, a young man, a great man, or a hoodlum. This is how the mask was used by actors in the Middle Ages and the Commedia dell'Arte.

Neutral masks (*masques noble*) – Jacques Le Coq

'The mask slows down the movement. The mask enlarges emotions by filtering out inessentials. The neutral mask (or masque noble) has no conflict within itself – only later in contact with the world does drama appear. The mask suspends movement under water. The mask supports melodrama (validates it). The actor wearing a neutral mask should try to make his own face assume the neutrality of the mask.'

It is important for the student to respect the mask, and the first lesson should teach how to respect it.

○ The mask should be put on by the student facing away from the audience or facing a mirror so that the preparation cannot be seen.
○ When the student is ready, they turn around, filling the mask with their body (mask neutral) or with the physical transformation of the characterisation of the character mask.
○ The student should put the mask on and stand still. They must think about the idea first without moving, and then, little by little, take a posture which expresses physically their environment (neutral mask) or the world which the character mask has created.
○ They must never speak behind a full mask.
○ After a while the teacher says 'Stop' and the student returns to neutral.

○ There can be a discussion from the observers and teachers which lead the person behind the mask to understand what physical messages they were giving off. It is better for the discussions to be negative so that the student behind the mask is not directed but has room to explore more possibilities. The student should find the gesture of the physical exploration of their world: it must not be imposed.

○ The student should never take the mask off to speak until the end of the exercise. Once they have finished the exercise, they must turn around with their back to the audience, take the mask off, and then speak.

○ To practice memory observation and precision the students can practise large single dramatic gestures such as:

> YOU!
> HALT!
> PEACE!
> AWAY!
> OH, ZEUS!

Go from gesture to gesture with no intervening movement; this will help the body to grow accustomed to economy of movement. Then try the following:

> Peel a lemon.
> Wipe a dish.
> Paint a picture.
> Untie a string.
> Shower.
> Knit.
> Arrange books.
> Carry a full or empty bucket.
> Fold a sheet.

There must be no symbolism or explanatory gesture. The student must move by the precision of observation and memory. Suggest the object by its shape, weight, fragility and roughness.

Further Than the Furthest Thing by Zinnie Harris, directed by Irina Brown
The cast had to imagine what it felt like to live on a remote island for many years. The people of the island would wait for a ship to come with provisions. I used a version of the neutral mask exercise, in which an actor puts on a neutral mask and then runs to the shore to wave to an approaching ship. The actor must get the captain's attention, or the supplies will not be delivered. The neutral mask takes away the actor's individuality, facial expressions and voice; they must learn to express that desperate intention solely though their body.

Classic LeCoq neutral mask exercises

The goodbye
1. The student puts on the mask, with their back to the rest of the class.
2. He turns around.
3. He is very late to say goodbye.
4. He runs to the end of the jetty as fast as he can.
5. He looks for his beloved.
6. He sees her.
7. He waves as the ship recedes into the distance.
8. He finishes waving when he can't see his beloved anymore.
9. He turns away.

Make sure the natural movements are enlarged to correspond with the mask. Make a definite stop at the end of the jetty. Sustain the change of focus as the ship moves further away. Make sure the dejection is over-emphasised.

The discovery
1. One or several students lie asleep (or in a state of non-consciousness) in a field or plain (make sure that the 'audience' can see the mask).
2. Awake and 'discover' the world: trees, water, animals, birds, flower, rocks, wind, sun, rain, grass etc. (nothing is surprising; it just is).
3. Choose any object – animals, rocks, birds etc. – and become this object. One acting area in the room will be the animal; when you move into another acting area, you will transform into a rock, and so forth. You will be neutral, then transform into a new form.

Variation 1
Change to action, for example, climb trees, pick flowers, swim in the water, etc.

Variation 2
Move and absorb the essence or qualities, rhythms, textures and pace of a city, in the morning, noon, and night.
>   You **cannot**:

○ Move your eyes.
○ Look at anything very close.
○ Be naturalistic.

The movement teacher can use these exercises a spring board to develop more exercises in imagination and exploration.

⊙ **Movement into practice: Twenty Movements** (DVD: Exercises 26 & 27)

Very often movement is used to warm up the actors to free and strengthen the body, breath, mind and imagination. The twenty movements is an exercise in using the strict form of the movements to stimulate the imagination and make a piece of theatre.

At the end of the second year, when the students have accumulated enough knowledge of pure movement and acrobatics, they are given the following exercise to embed the work into their body so that they own the movement work. The Twenty Movements is an exercise for the students to work on by themselves. They are given twenty familiar movements which they have to put together to make an individual piece of theatre. No twenty movements ever look the same. Although they have to be performed exactly to form, the twenty movements are as original as the student.

The students become aware of how hard it is not to add any embellishments, or mime, but to stick to a very clear physical text. The creativity comes out of the strict form. The piece needs to speak through the body, using space, rhythm, timing and story.

Example list of twenty movements

1. Full torso swing rise and lower (see p. 59).
2. Run and fly (see p. 65).
3. Run and fall.
4. Contre tension (x4) (see p. 65).
5. Diagonals (moving or on-spot) (x4) (see p. 21).
6. Figure of eight arm swing (x4) (see p. 63).
7. Lateral body swing (see p. 58).
8. ⊙ Any leap (a leap is one leg to the other leg) (DVD: Exercise 28).
9. ⊙ Cartwheel (DVD: Exercise 29).
10. Side roll (see p. 89).
11. Broken windmill (x4) (see p. 57).
12. Leg swings (x4) (see p. 61).
13. Rag doll swing (x4) (see page 57)
14. Shoulder roll (see p. 79).
15. Yoga spinal twist (see p. 83).
16. Leg lunge (see p. 80).
17. Pounce and pike (see p. 72).
18. Hip roll (see p. 69).
19. Undulations (see p. 33).
20. Any balance (see. p. 79, shoulder balance).

The rules

1. The movements can be linked together in any order, but only the movements on the list can be used as links.
2. There must be a dramatic use of space.
3. There must be a title suggesting the theme (or story).
4. There must be no mime.
5. There must be at least five supported vocal sounds.
6. There must be no music.
7. Rhythm, timing and breath can be used to tell the story, but the fundamental quality of each movement must not be adulterated.
8. Repeats can be split through the piece, can be done on one side, or can be done all in a row.
9. There must be no other additions.

The challenge is for the student to 'fill' the movements with imagination or emotion, and perform them in a particular order which conveys a story or theme. Some examples of titles could be: 'The Haunted House', 'Flying Home', 'Alice in Wonderland', or 'The Mermaid'.

9 Character mask

As with the neutral mask, character mask can be used as movement tool to help the actors with their physical transformation. Start the class with the pure movement and then introduce the mask work.

Here is an example of how to set up a mask class which can then be developed at the teacher's discretion.

1. Lay the character masks around the space and ask the class to go and look at them.
2. Choose a mask and hold it up in front of you. Get to know it.
3. Put it on your hand and watch it move around next to you.
4. Go over to the mirror and put it on your face.
5. Transform your body into the character which you feel the mask is.
6. Move away from the mirror and continue working the physical transformation of the mask.
7. Keep working to develop your character.

Ask one person in the group to choose a mask. They go over to the mirror and put the mask on (only they will see themselves). They walk to the top of the space and face the back wall. When they have transformed their body into their character they then turn around. The teacher then can ask the mask questions which will help the student to develop the character. For example:

○ What is your name?
○ How old are you?
○ What is your job?
○ Where do you live
○ What are your hobbies?

Clothes, wigs, hats shoes and props can be brought in by the teacher or the students to help the students discover their mask. As with the animal study, the student can become attached to their mask self!

Part 3

Body awareness, trust and sensitivity

10 Exploration of body and mind

Trust and sensitivity exercises

Trust

There is so much in acting about trusting the other person or people and it sometimes needs to be encouraged and learnt, especially in a new group of people. It can take only one member of the group to make a snide remark, or even just a look for another person to doubt themselves.

With a new class of students, I always discuss trust straight away, before any relationships have been established and the lack of trust has already set in and before the finger can be pointed at one person. I then do exercises, but exercises on their own will not work without the spirit of everybody wanting it to work.

These are a few examples of trust exercises. This first one is surprisingly difficult.

Exploring face and breath

1. Stand opposite another member of the group, shoulders down, arms by your side legs apart, on two feet. (All those things are essential to make sure the body language itself is not off-putting or threatening in any way.)
2. Study each other's face. Really study them and breath as if you are having a private conversation.
3. Don't hold your breath or stare out the other person.
4. Touch finger tips and then hold hands and then forearms.
5. One person shuts their eyes and the other explores their face, neck and hair.
6. Move onto another person with your eyes shut. Try to guess who they are.

The benefit of this exercise is that if a group of students can relax enough in each other's company to do this work, then when it comes to speaking closely in an intimate scene, or even just looking at each other in a free and emotional way, it becomes much more natural to do.

Exploring hands and fingers

1. Remove all jewellery and plasters. Roll up your sleeves
2. Divide the group into two lines standing opposite.
3. If the group has fewer men than women make sure you distribute them up equally between the two lines.
4. Everyone in group A stands with their hands out ready to receive the person standing opposite them in group B.
5. Everyone in group B places their hands in those of the person from group A who is opposite them.
6. Everyone in group A looks at the person opposite, and observes their face with their hands.
7. Once they remember which face goes with which hands, everyone in group A feels and explores the hands of the person opposite them, with their eyes closed, making sure not to go up into their wrists. (Hairy wrists can give the person away; notice how different the hands feel with the eyes shut than when they are open).
8. Spend about sixteen seconds exploring, then all group B moves up a person to be explored by the next person in group A.
9. Keep up the exploration until everybody has been explored.
10. Group A then spaces out around the room and closes their eyes.
11. Group B then creeps up to someone in group A and gives them their hands.
12. Group A then has to try to remember (by feel only and not through smell or voice), who that person is.
13. They whisper their name in their ear.
14. If they have got it right then the group B person squeezes their hands and then moves onto the next person.
15. If they get it wrong then the group B person stays there for longer
16. The group A person has three guesses and if they still get it wrong, move onto somebody else and come back later.

Variations

If the students in group A are doing well, the students in group B can try to bewilder them when they are guessing:

○ They can return to the same person from group A on several occasions.
○ They can try two different people with the right hand of one and the left hand of the other
○ The teacher could even go in and try to foil group A members

You can see who thinks outside the box!

11 Massage and relaxation

Massaging works at several levels in actor training.

1. With each student learning how to give and receive a massage they can help each other to get rid off any unwanted knots of tension.
2. It helps the students become free physically with each other's bodies.
3. It enables the students to have some calm in a busy week, and later in rehearsals and performance.
4. It allows the students to help relax each other's bodies, which in turn helps with the universal state.

How to massage

The massage discussed in this chapter has been adapted for the purpose of actor training. It is safe and specific and everybody can learn it.

To begin with, everybody keeps their clothes on but remove belts or sweat shirts which tend to ride up and are difficult to massage through. The process needs to be set up carefully so that it is still a group exercise, which will serve as group bonding as well as introducing the students to the benefits of massage.

1. Get into pairs.
2. One person lies down on their tummy on the mat, with their arms up by their head and their face on a jumper or cushion (option)
3. The second person either kneels at the side of them or, if more comfortable, sits on them just below their bottom, and not on their backs or legs (this helps prevent injury).

It is important for the pair to communicate their needs to one another, so that the right strength is applied. It is important that neither person is injured.

The rules

1. No talking, except for instructions for either person. (If there is a conversation or chat make sure that it is established at the beginning of the session, so that everybody is clear about the sort of atmosphere being set up. Conversations or chats should always be shared with the whole group so that it is part of the group bonding experience.)
2. The masseuse must never take their hands off the body. If you have to, always make sure one hand is left in contact with the body.
3. Breathe together (the whole class).
5. Meditation or relaxing music can be played.
4. Never stray from this routine as it is safe and good enough for the students' needs, as well as easy to time.

The massage

1. Place the hands on the base of the back or the top of the bottom and keep them there for a few minutes to warm the hands and to get used to the feeling of each other. Breathe together.
2. Start by effleurage.[3] Sweep the hands firmly and evenly up the back towards the neck, and round to the outside of the body, all the way round to the bottom of the back and up the middle of the spine and round again. Repeat this five times.
3. Take the hands to the lower back and the hips and sweep away with the heels of the hands, one after the other, ten times on the right side and then repeat on the left.
4. Effleurage the whole of the back again.
5. Find the base of the spine with the thumbs and then, without pressing on the bone, circle round the bone with the thumbs.
6. Next press firmly with the thumbs into different parts of the bottom and hips, semi-lifting the hips off the floor to relieve any pressure.
7. Effleurage the back again.
8. Lightly draw four lines on the back at the right of the spine as a guidance, imagining four channels of energy.
9. Place one thumb on top of the other and then press down and push up along the first channel of energy, up to the neck and out at the top.
10. Repeat this along all the channels and then repeat it on the left hand side of the spine.
11. Effleurage up the back on the right hand side, using the heels of the hand to add a little more pressure than the full back effleurage.
12. Take the flesh in big bunches and squeeze all over the back, like kneading bread.
13. Place the heels of the hands on either side of the spine at the top of the back and both people take a deep breath in.
14. On the out breath, press down firmly. There may be a bit of a cracking sound, but don't worry.
15. Work the way down the body to the bottom of the back.
16. Effleurage the back again.

---

[3] Effleurage simply means a stroking movement, used in massage.

17. Go to the top part of the back and, using the middle finger, push up between the shoulder and the neck, on the fleshy bit. This is where a lot of tension is held and therefore can be a bit painful sometimes. Listen to the other person so that it is clear how hard they require it.
18. Repeat on their left side.
19. Taking bunches of the same fleshy part, squeeze and knead the flesh between the thumb and all the other fingers.
20. Effleurage the back again.
21. Place the forehead on the floor (or jumper), then carefully massage the back of the neck.
22. With the finger tips massage the scalp, gently but firmly, squeezing the scalp, and the ears.
23. Sit to the right-hand side of the body and take the right arm. Massage all the fleshy parts of the arm, upper and lower. Massage the hand, digit by digit.
24. Repeat on the left arm.
25. Go to the right leg and effleurage the leg, firmly, not pressing on the back of the knees.
26. Knead the calf muscle and the thigh muscle, unless the person is ticklish when it is wiser to stick to the effleurage, so as not to make the person tense.
27. Turn the person over on their back and put their head in your lap.
28. Lift the head with one hand and massage the back of the neck with the other hand. Gently massage the face.
29. Massage the front of the legs (as with the back of the legs).
30. Finish by massaging each foot; in-steps and balls, heels and each toe.
31. Return the person to their tummy and lie across the bottom of the back and roll up and down over the bottom up to the neck and down towards the knees. Make sure you use the fleshy part of your body and not your bones.
32. Lie down long ways on the person you have massaged.

Massage and body manipulation in threes

This is taking the massage to the next level where the person who is being manipulated has to trust two people at a time. It also means that the two people have to work in conjunction with each other to enable proper manipulation of the passive person.

1. Get into groups of threes and have three mats for comfort.
    a. Person A lies on their back and relaxes completely, shuts their eyes and does not help at all.
    b. Person B sits at A's head and C sits at A's feet.
    c. B puts A's head into their hands and C holds onto A's ankles.
    d. B and C pull A's body in two directions along the floor (as if on a rack).
    e. B and C release A.
    f. Repeat three times.
2. B and C each take one of A's hands, as if they are shaking hands with them, and hold A's wrist with their other hand.
3. B and C gently move A's arm in its socket, loosening the wrist, elbow, shoulder.
4. B and C pull A's arms up towards the ceiling, as if they were pulling the shoulders out of their sockets.

5. B and C pull A's arms over A's head, slowly laying the arms parallel over A's head.
6. B goes to A's head, holding A's shoulders down.
7. C goes to A's legs, holding the ankles they sweep A's legs from side to side.
8. B massages the back of A's head and shoulders.
9. C massages the front of A's thighs and calves.
10. B and C turn A onto their tummy.
11. A claps their hands around B's neck, and B stands up, supporting A's armpits, stretching the back.
12. C lifts A's legs high up, pulling out of the thigh and releasing the spine. As legs are very heavy, B and C can have a leg each.
13. B massages A's upper body, and C massages A's legs.
14. B rolls up and down A with all their weight.
15. A moves into the folded leaf position, then tucks their toes under, rolling up through their spine, stands for a couple of minutes to feel the manipulation, then walks in space.
16. Repeat exercise with B and C taking A's position.

Relaxation

The use of voice is very important in this exercise, therefore I have not written it in point form, to avoid sounding 'jerky', as the aim is to get the students relaxed.

When the acting student gets tired in class or rehearsal and needs a rest, this is a very useful exercise which allows the body and mind to relax. It also assists with posture, using gravity to release and open the major joints, muscles and bones. Do this for twenty minutes with the eyes open or closed and at the end the student will feel invigorated and vital and ready for the rest of the day, usually a long rehearsal.

The way to relax

Lie on the back in supine (fully outstretched) or semi-supine (knees up facing the ceiling and with feet a little wider than the hips) and the arms open away from the body but with hands lower than the hips (this posture is good for those who feel discomfort in the lower back, when lying supine). Palms face upwards and if necessary, the head resting on a book or a jumper.

Use of a visualisation will aid relaxation, as in the following example.

Either close your eyes or keep them open if you prefer. Start by lifting your head off the floor, stretching the back of your neck to feel yourself lengthening your spine. Lower gently to the floor.

Focus your internal gaze between your eyes and let your jaw drop naturally, releasing your face. Breathe in and out through your nose.

Listen to as many distant sounds as you can hear, for example the aeroplanes, traffic noise, big red London buses, black taxis, and white vans; let it waft over you. Listen for activity in all the other studios. Try to hear voice classes, Laban classes and the improvisation classes' studios; imagine the receptionist, the facilities manager, and the secretaries, all focusing on their chores and activities. Let the feeling of relief that you are not doing these things wash over you, and relax. Know that you are having a little break, but your programme is waiting for you.

Listen to your thoughts. What are you thinking about? How does that affect your body i.e. tensions, fidgeting etc. Try to let them go. You can do this by imagining you are lying on a mountainside with your head in a mountain stream and the fresh, clear mountain water washing through your head. Let the stream take your thoughts down the mountain and into the sea; they will return, but for a moment you can escape them and you are able to concentrate on the present.

Now imagine that you are beginning to float above the floor. Your body is really light and starts to float through the ceiling and rise into the air, above your school or theatre, and you can look down and see it. As you rise higher and higher your school becomes smaller and smaller. You rise into the air above your country and onto a white fluffy cloud. The cloud is like a soft fluffy duvet and it flies you off, above the highest mountains, rivers and plains. It takes you under and around waterfalls and above the rain forests.

Continue until you get to a place that you have either been to before in your imagination, or in real life. It is a soft, cosy, warm sandy beach with yellow sand. You lie down on it with the turquoise sea lapping at your feet. There are green and ancient mountains all around and trees rustling behind you.

You begin to feel your body melt into the ground. Picture the sun shining deep into your body, melting it. Begin with your toes, in-steps heels and ankles. Move up to the shins calves, knees and thighs. Move up to the tummy and back and shoulders, and then finger tips, every digit of the hands and then the palms of the hands, the lower arms, the upper arms, the shoulders, the neck. Feel every part of the face begin to melt into the ground: the nose, the forehead, the ears, the cheek bones, the scalp and the hair. Feel as if everything has melted into the sand like melted butter.

Stay there for twenty minutes, which will enable the students to become refreshed.

Bring the attention back to the body and talk through each part of the body again, starting with the toes, then the in-steps, then the heels, ankles, shins, calves, knees and thighs. The bottom and pelvis, tummy and back, neck, shoulders, hands, lower arms, upper arms, face, head and hair.

Then imagine you are rising off the beach, above the beach, above the turquoise sea and above the water falls, rain forests, mountains, lakes and finally back home, above your country, above your school, in through the ceiling and above your space.

Fall down into your space and feel the floor.

When you hear the teacher's hand clap, squeeze everything as hard as you can; when you hear a click of fingers, release everything: let it all go! Repeat this a few times.

Take a big yawn and stretch and curl over on to the right side. Fold over into folded leaf and uncurl up through the spine (see spine work, p. 75).

Before getting up onto the feet do some leg stretches and some spine work. Take a deep breath and at the same time, bring the arms up and to the top, hands together; as you breathe out bring the hands to the heart centre.

Speak a line of text or a nursery rhyme so you can see where your breath is placed.

Blind lead

This exercise is useful on many levels. From the perspective of the blind person, it increases their sensitivity to space. It gives them over to another person, and it opens up their imagination, whilst heightening their senses. From the perspective of the leader, it gives them a certain amount of power and responsibility over the safety of another person. Additionally, it teaches them about space, and dealing with another person within that space. It encourages the way they touch and lead.

1. Stand next to someone.
2. Shake right hands and then put your left arm around the other person who in turn shuts their eyes.
3. Without speaking or assuring somebody vocally ('You will be alright!'), lead them with all the assurance of somebody leading a blind person, or an old lady across the road.
4. Keep going until they start relaxing, weaving in and out of the other people and making sure they are safe.
5. When they have started to feel more confident, then take your arm from around their waist and then hold hands like best friends. This is a bit like having a push-chair, where you have to be aware of the space between you and them and be even more careful.
6. Again, making sure they are all right, lead them around more quickly and start spinning and running.
7. Stop and ask the people with their eyes shut where the piano or door is.
8. Ask them how it felt.

Sometimes people feel that they are in a massive room or even some woods, while others feel cramped as if they are going to bump into other people.

Falling into each other's arms

Falling into each other's arms is useful because one person gives their physical safety over to many people. The person in the middle, with their eyes shut, will feel the energies of each person whilst they are being passed or finally thrown from person to person. They will feel who they prefer and trust in an instinctive way. The people on the outside will learn to work together, making the person feel safer. Smaller people will learn to open their legs for a firmer stance, and larger people will learn not to dominate with their physicality.

1. Start in a circle with one person in the middle.
2. That person shuts their eyes and crosses their arms over their chest.
3. The rest of the group has a wide, firm stance, one leg in front of the other and places their hands on the body of the person in the middle.
4. The person in the middle must keep their body firm i.e. not breaking in the spine, joints or pelvis.
5. They then fall back into somebody's arms.
6. That person gently at first pushes them into the next person's arms.
7. This builds up until the people round the edge do not all have their hands on the person in the middle.
8. The person can drop lower and lower

> **Health and safety**
> *The people on the edges need to open their legs wide and keep their backs straight. Their arms should be straight when the person falls into them and then they release down, bending their arms.*

☮ The impulse exercise (DVD: Exercise 30)

This is an advanced exercise which improves the more the student has individual control over each part of their body.

1. Work in pairs, A and B, standing opposite each other.
2. A shuts their eyes, stands in neutral and is very still.
3. B takes one finger and then places it on part of A's body and sends an energy through that part of the body.
4. A responds to the pressure accordingly, in an impulse movement (like a snail or slug contracting).
5. If B touches lightly then A moves slightly.
6. If B touches more vigorously then A retreats further.
7. B must not jab or push A, but send a laser-like energy through.
8. Every time A has the energy put through then they come back to neutral.
9. Swap over so that A is sending the impulses through B.

Variation

○ Repeat the same impulses, but this time A retracts but does not come up to neutral.
○ B has to get A all the way to a supine position without pushing or placing A in any way.
○ It can take a long time if done thoroughly.

Contact improvisation
Preparation

Firstly:

○ Stand opposite a partner, feet hip width apart and take hands with each other.
○ Lean back until the arms are fully outstretched, clasping hands firmly, but not squeezing.
○ Keep leaning back, but keep the head erect, looking into each other's eyes.
○ Bend the knees until the bottoms hover just above the ground and the arms are out-stretched.
○ Try it back to back.

Secondly:

○ Stand back to back
○ A lifts B up and over their shoulders. A lifts B by their arm pits and not the arms themselves. A must lift B's body up and out of their spine and lean forwards bending their knees and then finally placing their elbows on to their knees for safety.
○ A gradually bends down to the ground and slips the hips out from under them.
○ B, meanwhile, relaxes the entire time, trusting A.

Contact improvisation is a very good tool to enable the students to trust each other in a physical and psychological way.

It can be done in the most basic of ways and built up to use acrobatic lifts and falls, once the student has learnt those skills individually in a technically safe environment.

1. Get into pairs, A and B, preferably on a mat, for safety.
2. Stand back to back and lean in to each other. Close the eyes.
3. The teacher leads the session to begin with, just saying A or B. When A is called they take all the weight of B. A moves slowly bending their knees and moving their body, exploring all the possibilities of taking B's weight.
4. Change so B is now leading. Keep changing.
5. Eventually let it be free flow so that it can't be noticed who is the leader.
6. Try starting contact in different ways. But the weight has to be taken by the other person.
7. Get into threes or fours and then see if the whole group can manage it. Keep an eye on the group for safety purposes.

Part 4

Observation and imagination

In the following sections there will be a brief glance at some of the strands of movement, which are used as tools to encourage the observation, imagination and transformation. They are all extensive stand alone strands, which can be studied and used in a great deal more detail, depending on the needs of the groups and the interest of the teacher. For the overall training of the actor, however, it is most important to underpin every strand with the pure movement. This in turn keeps the body of the work flowing and develops the student's physicality to its full potential.

12 Observation

Imagination and transformation

It does not matter how much physical technique, alignment and release an actor has if they do not have any imagination and the power of observation. After all, physical technique, alignment and release do not make an actor. They merely free the actor of their habitual patterns and allows them to open up their inner selves. This then allows them to observe, imagine and take on the life and energy along with physical transformation of a character.

Once the actor has mastered the universal body, they can begin to observe characters and situations and learn about the impact on physicality. Early in the training, it is useful for students to experiment with copying each other's walks; first, the student should choose another member of the group to follow, and then they should attempt to emulate exactly that student's walk.

Emulating a walk

When to do this exercise

It is important to do this early on, before all the idiosyncrasies of a student's walk and posture have been ironed out. One of the most important discoveries is that the more tensions, blockages and idiosyncrasies you have in your body, the harder it is to transform into another's body shape. This is really a good exercise to do early on in the training to really understand, at least intellectually, the need for pure movement as a stepping stone to transformation.

There are several reasons why it is helpful for the students to observe each other:

○ They can see that, even if they copy somebody exactly, they do not necessarily look like that person. For example, a tall man may copy a small woman but could end up looking like an elegant man or a tall woman could copy a small woman, and end up looking like an old woman. So, one thing the students learn if that what you see is not always what transforms you.

○ It also allows the students to see that even if a member of the group can transform every muscle in their body physically, it is important to take on the presence, energy and life force of that person for it to look like a convincing transformation.

○ It also allows for the person who was being followed to observe their own physical posture, rhythm and walk when the transformer walks on their own inhabiting the new walk. It is important here that you make sure that the students are really clear that it is not a 'Mickey take' or a caricature, but a quick observation of the walk. If they were ever going to do this for a character in a play, they would spend more time and effort on it becoming their own, because if there is a lot of transformation work to do, it will take a lot of practice for the new one to become easy and stress free on their body.

1. First of all, get everybody to walk around the room, as near to their natural self as possible, considering they are in a movement lesson in bare feet, wearing black leggings and tee shirts or leotards.
2. When everyone has settled into a natural way of walking, then they should fall behind someone, so they are in pairs.
3. The person behind starts the copying of the person in front. The person in front must not change or add anything; it does feel quite odd and they can get self-conscious.

Make sure the person copying looks at certain things in particular:

○ The rhythm of the walk.
○ Where the weight is placed in the body and feet.
○ The placement of the neck and shoulders.
○ How turned out or turned in the feet, knees and hips are.
○ How do the shoulders and hands fall.
○ Where are the tensions or the releases

When everyone has done this, the group should sit down except for one couple. That couple carries on, and you can help the person behind try to master the walk, by clear, positive instructions.

Then the person whose walk it is observes, while the copier carries on by themselves. They really have to try to keep it going; it is very hard, because as soon as the other person has gone, unless it the walk is embedded deeply, it will disappear.

Try to encourage the students to do the change by their own observation rather than imposing too much from the outside, unless they are really struggling.

Everybody watches the person who had been observer walk around the room as the other person, changing back into themselves and then back into the person they were following, so the transformation is really clear.

Discussion
Questions to ask the person, who is doing it:

○ How does it feel?
○ Where are the tensions?
○ Do you feel like a woman (if it had been a man emulating a woman)?
○ Do you feel like the other person?
○ Does it make you feel more confident or less?

Questions to ask the person whose walk it was:

○ Do you think it looks like you?
○ Can you see how far your weight is back/forward, how stiff/floppy you are?

Be very clear with the class that when someone emulates another student's walk, it may look funny; that is not because the student has a 'funny walk', but because their walk is unique and matches their personality and body. There is nothing wrong with the way they walk. However, in the course of the training some of the quirks in their walk may be ironed out to allow them to reach the universal state. For example, if you walk with stooping shoulders, chin poked forward and waddle from side to side, the transition to a character with a gliding walk and stance which leans back will be much harder to achieve from that place than from a much more neutral place, hence all the emphasis on undoing physical habits, tensions and looseness.

Homework assignment

You can set the students this as a piece of movement homework to bring in to the next class. Ask them to choose three different people to follow, with the most extreme walks as they can. Make sure the person is not drunk or high on drugs, as the walks must not be peculiar due to foreign substances.

When they next come into class ask them to walk as one of the people, and then do the second, and finally the third. Then do one at a time from the corner.

In lines coming across the floor, do one walk and then change and change. Choose one of the walks and develop it in to a character. Imagine what sort of job the person would do and then, as the person start miming the work.

13 Animal study

The analysis of animal movement brings us closer to the study of the human body and helps with character creation. Because animals have bodies, feet and heads like us, they can be easier for the actor to approach than the four elements or materials, which can sometimes feel very vague.

Animal study is a movement study that can be done on many different levels and in many different ways. Its most obvious use is for the student to 'become' an animal as a means to making a physical transformation into a character. This could be as simple as a director saying to an actor, for example, 'I think this person you are playing is a rhinoceros', or 'this character is like a hyena'.

The actor can just try to remember what that animal is like, and then move around trying to be that animal, taking it into the human version as best as possible. They might even use television, DVDs, or internet movie websites such as YouTube to aid the transformation.

This is a good tool, but is really only fully used once the students have actually learnt how to observe real life animals, watching their weight, seeing or feeling their breathing, hearing their voice, and seeing or feeling) their skin or fur. Touching the animal, stroking them and feeling their mouth sucking or licking your hand or feeling a bird pecking or squawking near you, is a lot different to simply looking at it on a screen. However, there are obviously very few wild animals roaming around, so it is the students' responsibility to go to the zoo. It is imperative to make sure that the students watch television, DVDs and other technologies, so they can see the animals in their natural environment, observing their intra- and inter-species relationships, catching their own prey and looking after their young.

The work on animals is helped by the work on The Cat and dramatic acrobatics. As the students are learning The Cat, they are also learning the about the movements of the shoulder blades of animals such as lions and tigers, and elongation of the spinal column in animals such as meerkats standing on guard in the dessert.

The best research and clearest information come from David Attenborough's *Trials of Life* series; however there are lots of nature television programmes for children that are also suitable.

Animal study also allows the students to take on a complete transformation of an animal and, along with it, the total lack of self-consciousness that animals have. It is really good for an actor to not be worrying about what people think of the way they look, and to have a complete lack of self-consciousness. Studying animals in this way is particularly freeing, because animals will do everything in public that we humans would do in private.

Students should note the animals' contact with the ground, e.g. hooves could be likened to women in high heels, flat feet of bears could be those of an old man, the webbed feet of the duck could be the feet of a waddling woman. The slow motion of a three-toed sloth or chameleon could be ideal for a spy; the movement from relaxation to alert, defence to attack, is really good for an army or someone running away.

Animal study is also a very good way to teach the students to observe as an actor; to look at minute detail and to discover ways to make it look as if they are using four legs, legs that turn inside out, arms that are wings and necks that are six feet long, without actually having these actual physical attributes!

In actor training, it is good to make the animal study a project in and of itself. The student can therefore observe an animal and transform into that animal, without having to apply the traits to a character or text. The actor learns to transform in the simplest sense. It is what it is.

Movement in practice: animal work

This has been used in many Greek plays, such as *Ajax*, using lions and tigers for the warriors.

Decide on an animal which would suit the play and the chorus. For example, a pack of lions, meerkats or hyenas. Make the student become the pure animal, breathe, watch, listen, ready to pounce, ready to run, panting, strength and finally move the pack around the space as the animal.

Then take the properties of the animal and make them half animal and half human, sometimes this extreme works wonderfully for the Greek tragedy.

Another way of using animals would be to find the main character's animal and again work on it as a full animal, then bring it to half animal and half human, beginning to bring in some text and then finally wholly human but with the essence of the animal in the body, eyes, breath and voice. This can have a wonderful way of transforming the actor away from their own physical emotional rhythms to that of the character.

Teaching animal studies

The best time to start animal study is when the students have some idea of the workings of their own bodies, have begun to work on freeing, releasing and strengthening, so that whatever they observe in the physicality of the animal, they have a chance to make an approximate transformation.

If this work is done too early, the body will still be locked into personal patterns and shapes and will be unable to transform into an animal. However, it is important not to introduce this strand too late, because it can be an important 'break-through moment' in acting terms, and the student's performance in acting lessons will be helped by their newfound ability to transform. It can then be applied as the training goes on, and developed over the course of the actor's whole career.

There are many different ways of teaching animal study and, as with everything else, each teacher needs to find the way of teaching it that suits them. It is a good idea to get a year pass to a nearby zoo, so that the students can go there at least once a week during the project, and again in the following terms, including holidays, for additional research.

The pure movement work should be used as a basis for the animal work, just as with all the observational movement work. This is a way of using the pure movement, stretching and freeing the body, at the same time using it to help achieve paws, hind legs, suspension, release, weight, and space, but related to specific tasks and animal parts.

The student must have achieved a certain level of attainment in this work to be able to use it, otherwise there will be too much struggling with the technique of the pure movement, which will then mean it can't be used as a tool.

Each week set a task to observe, so that the students don't get bamboozled with too much information. Each week they will look at a different section of the zoo:

Week 1   A general look around to locate where the animals are housed.
Week 2   Primates.
Week 3   Big mammals.
Week 4.   Small mammals.
Week 5.   Birds.
Week 6.   Reptiles.
Week 7+   Really starting to study the chosen animal.

The lessons consist of the student researching the animal they are going to be working on. The student should keep a journal of their findings and observations, filling it with information, drawings and photos Start with a combination of the games (see games section, p. 3) and adapt them to suit the animals. Use the pure movement work, which should be executed properly and purely, and with the needs of the qualities of the animal that is being studied.

For example:

1. Rib stretches pure.
2. And then rib stretches imagining that the arms are wings, feeling the length and breadth and the feathers, or rib stretches as a primate, feeling the weight and length of their arms, or as a meerkat etc.

Teaching point

As a teacher, use your own observation to help enhance your own imagination to help the students.

You can use The Cat as a basis for the animal work. Of course, it is very good for big cats, or kittens, but it can be equally useful for trying birds, hyenas or three toed sloths.

All the work in pure movement is totally connected to the animal; for example, the flexibility in the spine matches cat movements, the movement in the shoulder blades matches that of lions and tigers, the elongation of the spinal column are like meerkats standing on guard in the desert. This is when acrobatics or gymnastics are not used as feats of virtuosity, but more to discover the basic organic movements of the animal.

There are some, for example, birds or komodo dragons, which take a lot of concentration and imagination, since their bodies are so far removed from human physicality and usage, but it is still a useful exercise.

After working on different groups of animals, start honing in on one animal.

This is when you need to decide what your aim is for the animal work.

○ Is it to stretch the students out of their physical comfort zone?
○ Or is it all right for the actors to choose their own animal, the animal which is nearest to themselves?

I would suggest that you let the students choose, up to a point, because they will work more at something they are inspired by, rather than something that is imposed.

If you have plenty of time, you could choose to do both, for example, one animal which works in the opposite rhythms to you – if you are a heavy set slow person, you could try a small scurrying animal and vice versa.

Things to observe and research in an animal study
○ Walking.
○ Breathing.
○ Weight distribution.
○ Muscle use.
○ How they stand, leap, trot or fly.
○ The spine.
○ Habitat.
○ Eating habits.
○ How they give birth and rear their young.
○ What animals are a threat to them.
○ What their contact is with the ground, and how it is different from ours?
  ■ Hooves, which trot, making only brief contact with the ground, like women in high heels.
  ■ Elongation of the spinal column like meerkats standing on guard in the desert.

Examples of animal classes

Class 1: Overview
Before the project starts, ask the class to go to the zoo, and for them to look at primates in particular. In the first class, ask the questions like 'Why do we do the animal project?', 'What did you learn at the zoo?' After a small amount of discussion, start the physical part of the class.

1. Play Ships and shores as a primate (see games section, p. 6).
2. Play Grandmother's footsteps as a primate (see games section, p. 10). Each time change the primate. Repeat the game, but this time incorporate the obstacle of chairs. When Grandmother turns around, the primates must get on to the chairs with both their hands and feet.

Class 2: Primates

1. Warm-up using pure movement, working particularly with the swings as there is so much swinging in primates' movements. As the students are doing this, they should imagine that they are the primate.
2. Space the mats out around the room and play pirates (see games section, p. 9) as primates. Use primate sounds from the beginning, and keep the primates as primates, even when they are out.
3. Play Grandmother's footsteps again.
4. Place the mats in a snake shape, and do a cat walk of primates.
   ○ Swinging the bodies from side to side.
   ○ Swinging the body through the arms.
   ○ Sideways gallop using the hands and feet (as if trying to get along branch).
   ○ Gallop along whilst one arm is pretending to carry a baby.
   ○ Leaping from mat to mat as if catching trees (sometimes monkeys just look and drop).
5. The class now works on their individual choice of primate, looking at posture, how it walks, runs, climbs, hides, attacks, eats, sleeps, wakes up and mates.
6. Split into small groups and watch each other. Discuss what they saw.

Class 3: Big cats

1. Discuss observations that students have made from the zoo and DVD footage.
2. Warm-up: Do some pure movement and The Cat, with cat-like qualities and sound, imagining paws, purring, kittens, claws.
3. Improvisation.
4. The class should now work on each of their individual cats, looking at the way they feed, watch, listen, breathe, sleep, wake up, walk, run, attack and play.

Improvisation

Play tango music and have the qualities of the big cats. Move on two feet around all the objects in the room, slinking and sliding through, over and under the objects. Circle around someone else, in twos looking at them, and sitting up on the knees as a cat, find the biggest yawn in a resting position. Flop down to supine position; shape the body into a cat shape. Find the placing of the paws, hind legs, the sighs and the tilt of the head, and go to sleep. Find the huge breath inside the huge body. Imagine the spine and the fur where it can be seen, find the qualities of being contained, ready, relaxed and alert. Imagine you are having a dream, and in the dream you are running across the African Plain. You see prey, for example a gazelle, wildebeest, or small baby animal. In your dreams you get to the prey and sink your teeth into it, and when you do turn over

---

onto your back, going back to sleep. Now you need a drink, you wake up, and you lick your lips with your big cat tongue. (Actually) go over to the water's edge, and take a long drink. See your prey on the horizon and go stealthily to the edges of the room. Make yourself quiet and small. Your muscles should be ready, and your intentions ready to spring and pounce. Try to get the prey with one big leap.

Class 4: Birds
1. Discuss the birds the students saw at the zoo, in the garden, parks, etc., and on DVD.
2. Warm-up.
3. Use the pure movement to find wings, flying, feet and heads.
4. Improvisation:
   - Chickens. Have feet like chickens. With hands behind your backs like wings, try to pick up jumpers, pens, and other objects with your chicken feet. Put something down for the students to imagine as food, and try to find a way of pecking the food.
   - Work on bigger birds with large open wings, stretching the head over the shoulder. Try to get the dirt out of the wings (cleaning themselves and getting rid of the old food.) Try putting your head under your armpit. Work on vultures, blue tits, chickens. Set up an improvisation, where there are chickens clucking and pecking in a farm-yard, and a cat comes along, and they all cluck away. Imagine the sensation of flying. Try to find the energy you need to fly, and the sensation of finding a current of air and gliding.
   - Eagles. Find the highest point in the room, for example the piano, wall bars or horse (make sure that it is safe). Imagine it is a mountainside, and grip the side of the mountain with your feet as an eagle. Look around you, owning the land – it belongs to you. Open your wings. Soar and float, then see an animal – catch it. Tear it apart with your claws and feet and beak; swallow it down, throwing it back.
   - Flamingos. Walk through water, picking your legs, stalking and parting your toes.
5. Group improvisation
   Split the group into two; one male and one female. Be birds of paradise or peacocks, and work out a mating ritual. Show the other group, and switch over.
6. Every student works on their own bird, as above.
7. Split the class into three groups and watch each other's birds.
8. The group discusses what they observed in each other.

Class 5: Small mammals
1. Students share their research of their particular choice of small mammal and their observations.
2. Warm-up.
   - Stuck in the mud (see games section, p. 9). When you are under the people's legs for safe-keeping, imagine you are in your little mouse house, and you cannot get tagged.
   - Cat and mouse (as meerkats).

3. Improvisation

Choose a small mammal and go about your daily life, for example, washing and eating. When the teacher bangs the drum, scamper back into the hole.

Class 6: Big mammals

1. Each student shares their research of the big mammals they chose.
2. Warm-up using the pure movement, as above.
3. Improvisations:
   - Find a space, and take the smallest amount of space you can in your body. Get bigger and bigger, until you can get the biggest amount of space in your body. Take the space; go back to small and inconspicuous. Become large again, and faster, and everyone has to get out of your way. Take long lumbering steps, have heavy floppy bodies, then heavy steps with held bodies. Gallop, side forward and back, covering as much ground as possible. Stop still.
     i. Giraffes
        Plant your feet and become as large and as tall as you can, trying to sweep your head on the ceiling, using undulations of the spine. Try to get around the room. Your tongue comes out, and you are trying to get the best leaves to chew. The top leaves are the best. As you are chewing, look around with your big giraffe eyes for predators.
           To get to get the feel of the height of the giraffe, the students can use the acrobatic movement of sitting on someone's shoulders (make sure they have spotters , i.e. people who stand by to make sure they don't fall and to catch them if they do.)
     ii. Camels
        Bring your body forward; you are a big bouncy camel. Arms hanging and furry, you are bad tempered. Stand opposite another camel, get into camel twos, and let it know that you do not like it.
     iii. Bears
        You are a bear scratching. Come onto your toes as a bear, try to balance, but you can't, so you flop back down onto all fours. Keep trying to get up onto two feet
     iv. Cows
        Be cows grazing in a field in Devon, chewing the cud and flicking flies away.

Class 7: Reptiles

1. The students share their research of the reptile which they studied.
2. Warm up, and in particular use parts of The Cat which are reptile like, for example, the leg kick, pounce and pike, and Indian push through.
3. Improvisation:
   - Walk around the space. When the drum is banged, run to an object in the room and become that object (so that if anyone walked in, it would look as if there were nobody in the room).
   - Repeat several times, and with different objects.
   - Get onto a mat and do constant, slow movement, rolling, moving on your tummy, without using your hands.

- ○ Find a position you could move from, move very fast and then stop.
- ○ Keep moving again, even slower.
- ○ Now your hands and feet have suckers on them, try to move around clinging and sucking like the rubber suckers on the surface of some soap dishes.
- ○ Lie on your tummy, using as much space as you can, imagining the sun is on every part of your body. Breathe and be still. Imagine the sand beneath you is hot and soft, and you start pulling yourself through the sand, using the power of your legs and shoulders, staying very close to the ground. Get into twos, catching flies. One person sits, the other person clicks their fingers behind them. The click is a fly; try and catch it with their tongue.

4. Group improvisation
   - ○ Half the class makes a physical structure in positions that they can hold. The rest of the group are any type of lizard or crocodile. They explore structure: all the nooks and crannies. Find some shade and wait.
   - ○ Each student then works on their own particular big mammal which they observed.
   - ○ Divide the group into three and watch each group.
   - ○ Discuss what they observe in each other.

After these general classes, the students can hone in on one animal. The classes can then be divided into a pure movement warm-up, followed by the students practising their own animal (having researched these qualities: walking, breathing, weight distribution, breath, muscle use, how they stand, leap, trot or fly, the spine. Also, habitat, eating habits, how they give birth and rear their young, and what animals are a threat to them).

It is useful to create a zoo or jungle habitat in the classroom if possible, using ropes, benches, mats and ramps. This can help to make the animal studies more thorough and convincing; for example, a student studying a chimp can feel what it is like to swing through the air.

Part of the study is to show the animals to the rest of the group. This can be done in several ways. For example, have the animals living in different rooms of the school and for everyone to walk around as though visiting a zoo. This means that the students should be in the moment and not have anything in particular planned or choreographed for the audience. Have the audience stay in one room, whilst the students show one animal at a time for about a minute each. This enables the students to plan and semi-choreograph their animal, based on earlier observation of what worked. The lesson is for the students to be able to repeat something exactly but for it to appear to be done for the first time. Another way is for students to work in family groups and to show each animal group together and to show how they work together, i.e. hunting, feeding mating and fighting.

14 Elements

It is essential for an actor to have the power of observation; they will be an even more powerful when the actor can use the observation and marry it with imagination.

The following movement tools are examples of ways in which the actor can use their observations of nature and the environment and, in the studio, filter those observations through the imagination to create distinct environment differences.

The elements are a fantastic way of really using the imagination to help the body transform, which in turn can be used by the actor as a means of characterisation.

There are many different ways of exploring the elements. It is important that the actor has observed the elements, before tackling them in the movement lesson. Because the elements have been experienced by most people, they are generally instantly available to the students' imagination; for example:

○ Everybody walks on the ground.
○ Everybody breathes the air.
○ Everybody has seen some kind of fire, be it a bonfire, a candle or a fire in a grate.
○ Everyone has experienced some form of water.

However, if the student is required to use an aspect of an element in more detail to create the world of a play, or in their own physical transformation, it is more important to go and look at the sea, a pond or a lake and ideally swim in it, or to visit a waterfall, rapids or mountain stream if the student needed to physicalise any of these. In the same way it would also help to go walking in a heavily muddy field or on concrete or a beach of sand and feel the real differences to how your body feels when experiencing the weight of the mud, and the different properties of the sand if the student was required to physicalise any of these properties.

🎴 Element exercises (DVD: Exercise 31)

Earth
Exercise 1

1. Sit in a circle and one person takes an imaginary piece of clay.
2. They roll it into a ball and start shaping it with their hands into something realistic, for example a mobile telephone.
3. When it is moulded they use it and hand it on to the next person who also uses it to show they know what it is. They then remould the telephone into something else, for example, a banana.
4. If the second person didn't understand what it was they hand it back to the first person who tries again.
5. Go around the whole circle.
6. On the second time round make it a much bigger piece of clay so the class has to get a lot more physical i.e. cars, space hoppers, kites etc.

The students should try hard to imagine what the clay feels like; is it heavy? Sticky? How difficult is it to mould?

Variation 1
- Do the same in pairs.
- Repeat in threes and fours.

Variation 2 – Improvisation
- Start walking around the space as if you are walking along a road on a bright sunny day.
- The road leads you to the countryside and the walk takes you into a field (feel how the body changes when walking along a grassy, tufty field).
- The grass gets thicker and thicker and your walk changes accordingly.
- The grass turns thin and a little muddy.
- It gets very muddy and there is no grass left. Your walk changes accordingly.
- As the mud gets thicker it goes up to your ankles.
- Then your knees and then your thighs and finally up to your neck.
- It is very hard at this point to keep moving but that is the rule, you have to keep moving.
- Eventually the mud goes over your head, but you can breathe and you have to move.
- Keep walking around the room like this and eventually you can feel the weight of the mud in your body.
- You are a mud person.
- Find a way of greeting the other mud people in your class.
- Find a way of speaking as a mud person.
- Eventually become a human, but with the element of earth in your whole body.
- Ask the question, 'What character would have this element?'

Exercise 2 – improvisation
1. Lie on the floor in any shape you like.

2. Imagine you are lying on the bed of a forest.
3. You can feel the soft earth and pine needles under your body.
4. After a while, feel as if you are melting into the earth.
5. You are getting deeper and deeper into the earth's surface and then the crust of the earth.
6. You are going through the many layers of the earth's surface until you get to the centre of the earth.
7. What do you imagine it feels like?
8. Start moving in the way you imagine it would feel.
9. Add sound.
10. If you come across another piece of the earth then join up with it.
11. Keep moving around the space until you are all joined up and the whole group is moving as the centre of the earth. This can also be done as a group movement session.
12. Peel gently away from each other and then lie still.
13. Roll over to folded leaf and then tuck your toes under and uncurl through the spine.
14. Walk around now as people; you will feel how 'earthed' you are.

Variation – improvisation
Group work
Get into groups of four or five and make up a group body of earth and show it to the other groups. For example:

- Earth in a flower pot.
- A sandy beach.
- A muddy field.
- Clay on a potter's wheel.

Water
Improvisation
1. Imagine you are walking along a sandy beach.
2. You have the breeze in your hair and you can see for miles on the horizon.
3. The sand is dry and you can feel it running through your toes.
4. You get nearer to the water's edge and the sand becomes wetter and your feet start to sink into it.
5. You start walking along the edge of the beach and the water is now up to your ankles.
6. Turn and face the sea and start walking into it.
7. Firstly up to you calves; how does that make you walk?
8. Then your thighs.
9. Then your waist, when you start feeling the need to swim.
10. Then up to your chest.
11. And finally over your head, but you can breathe.
12. You then start moving about in the water until you start becoming the water.
13. Your whole body dissolves into the water and everybody floats around as if in the sea
14. You get deeper and deeper until you are the centre of the deepest part of the sea.

15. Find a sound that matches the centre of the sea.
16. If you meet up with another person, join in their sea and see if it changes.
17. A shoal of fish comes swimming through you.
18. A big whale comes swimming through you.
19. Start getting higher up and so you are more affected by what's above on the surface – the weather, the ships, and the motor boats.
20. Move as if a motor boat has just gone over the surface.
21. Calm down.
22. Move as if a big sailing ship has passed over the surface of the sea.
23. Now a storm is brewing and you are the waves in the centre of the sea and it gets choppier and choppier and the waves get more and more violent.
24. You then build the storm with the whole group is working together and then you start crashing onto the beach.

Ask the class to form a group which represents the tide, crashing onto the beach, and then pulling back through the gravel and sand and rippling out into the sea. The waves can get more frantic, as in a storm, or can calm down until the whole group is a gentle sea, rippling in the sunlight.

Variations – improvisation
Group work
Divide everybody into groups of four or five and ask them to make their own body of water. For example:

- A waterfall.
- A waterfall going into a rapid.
- A rapid.
- A toilet flushing.
- Water going down the plug hole.
- An icicle melting and dripping.

Example

In *Further Than the Furthest Thing* (by Zinnie Harris, directed by Irina Brown at the National Theatre, 2000) the above imaginative experience was used to give the actors the feeling of wading into a lake. The opening scene of the play required a man to wade into a lake and take a swim even though there was no water in sight. I worked on the whole cast moving in water to set up a feeling of ensemble, before we honed it down to the character actually taking the swim. He also, incidentally, had to be thrown around by a volcano, so I introduced him to some acrobatic movements, such as side rolling and shoulder rolling to achieve this effect.

Fire
Improvisation
1. Stand on your own.
2. You are a sparkler on bonfire night, and I light you – what happens?
3. After you have explored the sparkler as a sparkler, turn it into a person. What type of person acts like a sparkler?
4. All the sparkler people move around greeting each other. What kinds of speech do the sparkler people have?
5. You can make up gobble gook as your own language.
6. Choose a firework and then I light you. What happens? Use lots of sound as well movement.
7. A candle flame. I light your wick and you are a candle flame flickering in the night. Watch it for a while.
8. Become the candle flame.
9. A star shining all over the room.

Group work 1
1. Start in a big pile as if you are a pile of twigs and branches.
2. Light a toe in the pile.
3. The fire travels through the pile and eventually the whole group is lit.
4. The fire begins to get more and more out of control and flames shoot up into the sky; they crackle and spit and roar (plenty of vocal work for this).
5. Eventually the fire starts dying down until it's just a glowing ember.
6. The students peel off and walk around as people who are glowing embers with the odd spark from time to time
7. Ask the students what kind of person they are.

Group work 2 – improvisation
In groups of four or five, ask each group to make a type of fire. They need to have a beginning, middle and end. Practise it, show it to the other groups. They have to guess what type of fire it is.

Air
Exercise 1 – improvisation
1. Find a space on your own.
2. Lie in whichever way you choose. You are a deflated balloon at a children's party. I have just opened the bag and scattered you all over the room.
3. I am now going to blow you up, little by little.
4. You have lots of air filling your body, growing larger and larger, more and more filled with air.
5. When you are inflated all the way and all of your body (including your feet) is filled with air, you try to find some way of hovering, like a filled balloon at rest.
6. In comes a gust of wind and blows you.
7. Try to waft around the room. When you knock into other balloons, really try to feel like a balloon does.
8. Make sure the air is in your face and mind too.

9. After a while I will pop you and you BANG and drop to the floor.

10. Alternatively I may pull out your knot so the way you deflate is entirely different.

11. I may ask you to have a slow puncture, which again is another entirely different way of deflating.

Variation

After exploring the balloon, try becoming air like people. What is your laughter like? What is your job? What is your walk like, your hand movements, your knees and your breath?

Exercise 2 – improvisation

1. Lie on the floor all over the space.

2. You are a duckling feather, which has just moulted from a duckling.

3. You are caught in a tree and there is a small wind.

4. Eventually the wind gets a little stronger and you are set free from the tree.

5. You are blown about the space.

6. You land.

Try turning this into people, again asking the class what kind of person they are? How old? What is your laugh, cry and general disposition like?

Exercise 3 – improvisation

Group work

1. Get into small groups. Each group makes up a type of air. They rehearse it with sound and breath, and then show it to the rest of the group to guess what it is. Some ideas are as follows:

    ○ A hurricane.
    ○ A whirlwind.
    ○ A gentle breeze.
    ○ A storm brewing.
    ○ A vent of air.

Movement in practice

Medea (by Euripides, adapted by Liz Lochhead and directed by Ian Wooldridge at the British American Drama academy). The director, Ian Wooldridge, set the play in an empty space with only a black and white chequered floor. The costumes were simple so the story needed to be told through the body, in transformation, as well as spatially. As Ian wanted a fluid and dynamic series of images, my work involved, conducting workshops which focused on the elements.

As there was a Scottish flavour to the play, I worked on the elements of earth and air in particular. I used the imagery of the mountains with heather under the feet and the feeling of driving wind and lashing Scottish rain. Because many of the students came from urban environments with virtually no experience of open space and countryside, it was essential to kick start their imaginations into a rural sensory experience.

Part 5

Imagination and transformation

The actor needs to be able to use not only observation, but also imagination, and ultimately transformation. The following are movement exercises to help develop the actor's ability to inhabit their observation and imagination into physical transformation.

15 The Seven Deadly Sins

The purpose of exploring the Seven Deadly Sins in a physical way is directly related to a character the actor is studying. Although when explored in a movement class or rehearsal, they are done in an exaggerated way, they are still all things at extreme levels which all people feel at some time. They are done in this manner so that the actor can show what impulse they are having. When used in acting, it will only be the essence of the deadly sin which will be left.

Students explore the physicalisation of the psychological aspects of the Seven Deadly Sins. The play *The Tragical History of Dr Faustus* by Christopher Marlowe can be used in the classes as inspiration for the students.

1. Pride.
2. Avarice.
3. Envy.
4. Wrath.
5. Lust.
6. Gluttony.
7. Sloth.

Health and safety
Make sure that the students are very physically warmed up; put mats out for their physical safety and be on the lookout for psychological safety as some students can become upset at having to go to an extreme emotion place. Anger, in particular, can be hard to control.

Pride

Pride and vanity are competitive. If the way other people judge you really bothers you – or if you feel that you are better than those around you, you have a lot of pride. The opposite of pride is humility. Seeing ourselves as we are and not comparing ourselves to others is humility.

How to physicalise pride

1. Get into groups of five.
2. One person walks around the space, completely ignoring everybody else, and being totally self-obsessed. The rest of the group play Humility. So as Pride is walking around, head in the air, Humility is rushing around them sweeping the dirt from under their feet.
3. Pride does not know Humility is there. Humility is so humble they just want to make Pride's life better.
4. The students should be encouraged to find ways of developing this idea, getting the feeling of Pride running all the way through the body, in particular the spine.
5. Change people, so that each person has an opportunity to be Pride and Humility.

Avarice/greed

Greed wants to get its fair share or a bit more. Generosity is the opposite of greed; it is letting others get the credit or praise.

How to physicalise avarice

1. Decide on something you really want. See an object in the room which you want more than anything in the world. Do anything you need to get it. If you get it, then try to get some other object. Want them all; keep them all. Get the feeling of greed and never being satisfied running all the way through the body, spine and limbs.
2. Do the opposite and be as generous as you can. Give away everything you have.

Envy

Envy resents the good others receive or even might receive. Love is the opposite of envy. Love actively seeks the good of others for their sake.

How to physicalise envy

1. Lie on the mat and think of someone who has got something you want. The acting job you wanted, the adulations they received for some work which you thought was for you. Let let the feeling seep through your veins, spine, head and limbs and then start moving the body in relation to the feelings.
2. Writhe around, pull the hair out. Feel it pushing up through the spine.
3. Make sure, however, that the movement is in response to the emotion and thought and not a plastic movement like a dancer.
4. Do the opposite of envy. Be love. Walk around the space and be in love with everybody and everything. Feel love and react physically to the feeling of love. Move the body in reaction to the feeling.

Wrath/Anger

Anger is often our first reaction to the problems of others. Impatience with the faults of others is related to this. Kindness is the opposite of wrath (taking the tender approach).

How to physicalise wrath
1. Sit on a mat and start thinking about what makes you the angriest.
2. Move the body in reaction to the emotion.
3. Think about when you are really angry and do with your body what you would like to do to show how angry you are, or what you would like to do to get rid of the angry feelings.
4. Travel it across the room trying to get to the other side with the angry movement.
5. Physicalise the opposite, kindness. Think of when you felt the most kind, and move the body as you would if you could express kindness through the body.

Lust

Lust is the self-destructive drive for pleasure out of proportion to its worth. Self-control is the opposite of lust. Self-control and self-mastery prevent pleasure, which are controlled like a muscle.

How to physicalise lust
1. Move around the space lusting after everything and everybody.
2. Make the body react physically to the feelings of lust. You want and lust after something. You feel it in your fingertips, you feel it in your lips and tongue, but the lust is never satisfied.
3. Do the opposite of lust: self-control. See something you want more than anything. Look at it, want it, and then walk away, with the feeling of self-control running through the spine. Everything tightens up with self-control
4. Get into pairs. One person is lust and the other is self-control. Then switch over.

Gluttony

Gluttony is when someone cannot get enough of something, for example, food. However, it does not just relate to food, but also entertainment and even the company of others. The opposite of gluttony is temperance.

How to physicalise gluttony
1. Sit on a mat and imagine that there is the biggest banquet of food awaiting you.
2. Start eating it, enjoying it, feel what is happening to your body. It's getting fuller and fuller and you eat more and more. The food is running down your face, down your body, you keep stuffing the food in. You are sick and then you carry on eating.
3. Do the opposite of gluttony: temperance. Look at the banquet of food in front of you and resist. Do not eat it. Look at it and want it but do not have it. Remember the feeling of resisting something you want and physicalise that.

Sloth

Sloth is when a person cannot be bothered to do anything at all. The opposite of sloth is zeal.

How to physicalise sloth

1. Lie on the floor and feel really heavy.
2. Try to remember how it feels to need to do something but not being able to be bothered at all. For example: think of trying to get out of bed in the morning, having the need to get up, but not being able to muster the energy. You have to move. You have to try to get up, so it is not a comfortable state to be in. It is not like going back to sleep.
3. Physicalise the opposite, zeal.
4. Have lots and lots of energy and rush around fulfilling lots of things.

16 Explorative movement

Creative, imaginative and explorative movement

Explorative movement uses the power of the imagination to affect the body. It is not enough just to imagine something in the mind; we have to let that image filter down through every fibre of the body, with truly transformative results. The following exercises help the actor to enter the world of a particular play and/or character physically, thus supporting the work they do in rehearsals.

Very often the feeling the actors get after a creative explorative session is that they have become a different human being, influenced by the textures or qualities that they have explored in the class. This is the end-result of observation; though observation is one of the most important skills for an actor, it is the ability to physically embody these observations and ideas that makes a real transformation.

Explorative movement is also a great way to get the cast of a play together as an ensemble and to explore together whatever the physical world of the play requires, it may be a matter, a time in history, a country, which has a certain type of quality which can be physicalised before text is added.

Group movement and improvisation

These exercises are a way to really get your group working together in a very imaginative fashion. They are also good for auditions to see how people work in a group, or as class exercises to build up thought with imagination, or for a rehearsal of a play where these exercises can develop in rehearsal.

These exploratory exercises can be done at any level and at any place in schools and actor training.

Mickey Mouse movement

The student takes a speech they are working on and on every word physically inhabits or mimes, in an exaggerated way, the meaning of each word. This will enable the student to understand fully the meaning of the text and when the exaggerated movement is removed, the essence of the mean in left in the acting.

The journey

One person makes a huge physical body shape and the next person moves through the gaps in the body and then makes a shape which contacts physically. A third person goes through the gaps in both people and then attaches themselves on to the second person. Once the group have mastered this, they can imagine that they are escaping from a prison or exploring the undergrowth.

The sea monster

Divide the class into groups of five to seven. Each group contacts physically in as many ways as possible and makes a sea monster. The monster then must be still and quiet. The group making up the monster must find a group breath. The monster is asleep in his cave next to the sea. It wakes up and feels very hungry; the group starts finding ways of moving as one being. The monster must try to keep the same breath and rhythm and not have anybody sticking out as the one human within the monster. It can move in whatever way the teacher or leader of the audition prefers; for example, the monster travels along the sand in search for some food. It has to climb over a rocky cliff, and then down into a deep and muddy hole, only to come out at the other end, where, all covered in mud, it finds its prey and then devours the lot before slipping into the depths of the ocean for an lovely after-meal nap. After several moments of calm it suddenly bursts out of the sea as it is interrupted by a motor boat and has to scamper quickly back to its cave where he finally can get some rest!! An alternative ending would be for it to go to sleep on the surface of the sea like a great big jelly fish.

In an audition, people may think the idea is to be noticed when, in fact, it is to be part of the group. This exercise is also good for the ensemble as again it is about imagination and blending with the group.

The machine

You can either decide what the machine is for and then make it accordingly, or you can make the machine, and then decide what it is for. Remind the students that their movement should not be too complicated or difficult because they are only small cogs in a much larger machine, and they need to keep the movement going or the machine will break.

1. One person goes into the space and starts a machine-like repetitive movement and sound.
2. Add another person, and they either go in rhythm or a contrary rhythm.
3. Keep adding people into the machine until it is entirely working.
4. When it is all working you can have two control knobs: one volume and one speed.
5. See if they can speed it up (5 being medium, 10 being full speed) and slow it down to 3, 2, 1 until it is completely at a stand still.
6. Likewise the volume 5 being medium, 10 being fast and 1 being the quietist.

Tableaux

Start with dividing the group into two halves. Each half decide on a scene that includes that many people. For example:

○ Scene of an accident.
○ Wedding.
○ Birth.
○ Christening.

1. Group A stands with their eyes closed. Each member of group B takes charge of a person from group A and moulds them into a character in that tableau or 'frozen picture'.
2. When group A has finished, and still with their eyes shut, each member of group B explains what position they are in to the rest of their blind group; they can even guess what they are doing.
3. As everyone explains, the jigsaw is put together and the group guesses.
4. If they get it right they open their eyes and improvise the scene.

Physicality for characters
Improvisation
1. Everybody lies on the floor and relax.
2. As you are relaxing you run through the story of the play in your head.
3. Then think about your character and where they were born.
   ○ Think about what kind of parents they had. Were the parents still together when you were born? What kind of relationship did your parents have with each other and what kind of relationship did they have with you?
   ○ Were you born at home or hospital or even in a field or the back of a car?
4. Now imagine you are being born.
   ○ Who is the first person to hold you? Are you born into a big family? Do you have brothers and sisters?
   ○ Are you oldest, youngest, middle or smallest child?
   ○ Is your father at home? Is he in work?
   ○ Does your mother work?
   ○ Who feeds you?
   ○ What sort of baby are you
   ○ Do you cry a lot or are you quite quiet?
5. Start moving and crying like the kind of baby you are.
6. Grow up to the toddler you are; what kind of toys do you play with? Who else is in your life?
7. Keep the improvisations going until you reach the age of the person you are in the play. This will really help if you have some kind of disability or an aging issue, or gout, because as you are going through the improvisation, you will be able to see where the problem in your body started.
8. When you have reached the age of your character in the time-frame of the play, you will be better able to play that character fully − rather than just playing their age, their disability or their dramatic function. Once you have 'found' this character you can move on to other improvisations.
9. Wake up in the morning and do their morning preparations, really thinking about whether they are taking a bath, shower or just getting into their clothes.
   ○ Do they have a dresser?
   ○ What about breakfast?

○ Where do they have it and with whom?

○ What do they do during the morning and leading up to lunch?

○ What do they have for lunch and where do they have it?

○ What do they do after lunch and the lead up until dinner?

○ Carry on with the improvisation until bed time and then go to bed.

○ This can take up an hour or more and is well worth doing, as it really gives the actors some time to really focus on their physicality.

(This also links to Stanislavski's method of acting; he believed that the actor should always know what their character had for breakfast!)

Elegance

Often a director will want to work on style and elegance. The following improvisation has worked successfully for plays set in the 1920s or 1930s.

1. Imagine you are in a large mansion and you have all arrived for a ball or a weekend party.
2. You have all come back from riding or walking and you have all retired to your rooms.
3. You are lying in a luxurious bed, with satin sheets.
4. You are lying naked, so you can really feel the luxury of the satin or silk on your skin.
5. You have left the curtains open and one of the large bay sash windows and there is a warm breeze blowing gently into your room.
6. There is an apple blossom tree heavy with pink blossom, waving in your open window.
7. You have drifted into a lovely afternoon nap, so you will be up and ready for your evening party.
8. You wake up to the sound of the birds; the sun is going down.
9. You pad across luxury velvet carpet to close the windows and the heavy satin curtains. Before you do that you let the evening breeze waft over your naked body.
10. Go to your en suite bathroom, with the roll top bath and black and white tiles and free-standing wash stand.
11. You run a hot deep and heavily perfumed bath with Chanel bubbles floating in it.
12. You go over to the gramophone record player and put on soft music to get you in the mood for the evening.
13. You climb into the bath and lie down, close your eyes and let the music and water float over your naked body.
14. After a while, a servant comes in and washes your hair, giving it a gentle massage and condition, and gives you a facial.
15. They leave you to soak with the hair conditioner in and the face pack on your face.
16. As you are lying there you hear the gentle sound of them getting your clothes ready and laying them out on the bed for you.
17. They then come back in and remove your face pack and pour clear warm water from the big jug all over your head and body.
18. You climb out of the bath and you are wrapped in a big fluffy white bath towel.

19. You sit down on a golden guilt chair and the servant starts to manicure your hands, massaging cream into them, up to your forearms and upper arms and shoulders and neck, and filing your nails. They then start painting your nails or for the men buffing them up to a stunning shine.

20. They then move to your feet and give you a pedicure and foot massage and file your toe nails and polish or buff your toes.

21. They then massage your calves, shins and thighs.

22. They then start drying your hair, curling, twisting, or straightening it for the ladies and 'Brylcreeming' it for the gentlemen.

23. They then start applying makeup for the ladies and the men are given a wet shave, with a brush and lather.

24. They finally add lipstick for the ladies and moisturiser for the men.

25. Get up and let your soft fluffy white towel fall to the floor.

26. Step into silky underwear and seamed silk stockings (socks and garters for the men).

27. Climb into a long floating satin gown (dinner suit and bow ties for the men).

28. Step into high, but comfortable strappy sandals for the ladies and highly polished leather brogues for the men.

29. Spray on the most expensive perfume or after shave that you can find and go and look at yourself in a long mirror.

30. Finally, ladies drape a fox fur round your neck or a silken scarf and light up a long mint cigarette in a ebony cigarette holder and put your lipstick, a handkerchief and your cigarette box in your little gold clutch bag.

31. And men put a handkerchief in your top pocket with a comb and check to see if you have plenty of cigarettes in your cigarette box and a lighter that well and truly works. Put a white scarf around your neck.

32. Ladies wait for your man to knock on your door and men make sure you arrive at the door with some jewellery or a flower for your lady.

33. Ladies wear it and then take the man's arm and sweep down the curved staircase (think Fred Astaire and Ginger Rogers).

34. Walk around shaking hands with everybody and being formally greeted by your host.

35. Ladies retire to the powder room and men go and start drinking and smoking, laughing and talking.

36. When the ladies return, the men stand up and give the ladies a sherry or a gin and tonic.

37. They then talk and laugh and go into the dining hall for a long and elegant dinner.

38. Make sure you spend some time on this before the men retire to the salon for cigars and brandy and the ladies go to the powder room.

39. Music is then heard in the ballroom and everybody goes in for a big dance.

40. Waltzes, quadrilles, fox trots, tangos and polkas. (If the students know these dances, great, if not play the music and by this point they should be able to improvise quite well, make sure the men are leading though.)

41. After a long night, end with a slow waltz, before retiring to your rooms.

For modern actors, this helps them to feel the pace and luxury of 1920s life, and to embody that class and elegance, so that they connect more deeply to their characters. Sometimes it is useful to put on appropriate music from the time, as this will give the actors more inspiration for the rhythm and style of their movement.

A fan is as useful a tool for the women as swords and canes are for the men. The fan can be held, it can hide, reveal, draw attention, or repel; it can punctuate a phrase or draw it out lingeringly. The actors can use this teasing, tantalising resource. There was an entire pantomime language of the fan, with specific meanings attached to specific gestures: 'We are watched', 'Follow me', 'I love another', and many more.

The grid

1. On your own, walk in straight lines up and down the room.
2. Walk down one length with an exaggerated physical trait, for example, your head poked forward.
3. Turn a sharp corner and change the physical trait, for example, heavily bent knees.
4. Turn a sharp corner again and change again the physical shape, for example, elbows flapping.
5. Change again, and maybe this time turn your hands round and round.
6. Keep this going and then see if you can remember the sequence.
7. Keep repeating it until it is second nature to you.
8. Then add two of them together, for example, the poking head and the flapping elbows.
9. Then the bent knees with the curling hands.
10. Then add all four until you have a person who has bent knees, flapping elbows, curling hands and a poking neck.
11. Watch each other.
12. Learn each others.
13. Have a whole town of these interesting looking people walking on these grids.
14. Make the people become as real as possible
    - What job do they have?
    - What work do they do?
    - Where do they live etc?

17 Period movement

An overview of period movement by Michael Gaunt

An actor in their time is likely to encounter a wide repertoire of plays written at various times in different centuries. The actor will be aware of a plethora of plays and scripts, some with contemporary settings, some with a retrospective look at the past. A range of production and presentation styles will be encountered that may reflect the period in which the play was written, or, they may be concept-driven to gain a fresh insight into a play, or in an attempt to make the play relevant to the present time. For example, in successive centuries Elizabethan plays have had their texts adjusted, added to, or reduced to suit a director's or leading actor's concept, to introduce an 'improvement', or a change in the period setting. At other times a play is scrutinised through a fashionable political lens sometimes resulting in a narrative 'through line' deviating from the playwright's original design and intention.

Nevertheless, when studying a play written in a past period, an actor may wish to explore the world of that play and the people living in it to gain an understanding of its historical context, and to imagine the demands of life at that time, a character's place within the society in which they lived. The research will raise countless questions. What sort of family have they been born in? What is the family's social status and does it change within the action of the play? What does the character do in order to live? Do they have enough to eat? What is the character's age: state of health and life expectancy? How are these factors reflected in a character's physicality and movement? What are the existing social norms of belief: religious and political? What standards of behaviour have been learnt, is a character mannered or unmannered? What do they believe in and of what are they fearful? Do they believe in God? Do they fear for their immortal soul, for the souls of loved ones? Are they fearful of medical quackery, of invasion, homelessness, starvation? How do they use their bodies in daily life? How does this affect them physically? How does it show in their movement? Do they work physically on the land on the land? Is a man in the army or navy of the day and what does, or did, this involve? Is a woman worn out and weakened by childbearing? Does a woman have the benefits of servants, or is she an intelligent woman without material resources, as imagined by Charlotte Bronte in her novel *Jane Eyre*? What are the modes of travel and does an individual's life involve extensive walking, or horse riding? What levels of physical strength and endurance do they possess? Can it be assumed a modern man or woman possesses comparable levels of physical strength and endurance?

These factors and many others may influence a character in terms of mental well-being, physical expression and movement; what is felt emotionally is expressed in a person's physicality – the psycho/physical state at key moments in a character's life. A significant question to be answered is what is different in the 'now' experience of life for the characters within the world of the play, compared to the 'now' experience of the actor living in the world of today? Understanding these differences can be significant when making characterisation choices. Preparing and studying a character who lived in a specific period of time can advance and consolidate an actor's understanding of prevailing social behaviour and rules of etiquette. Without personal preparation the alternative is to rely entirely on a playwright's instructions and a director's explanation.

The working actor ideally should maintain an awareness and practical understanding of their body, its flexibility and movement capability, and how it might be used in a characterisation There is, of course, no one way to start building a character. Should the actor start by focusing on what is similar between the character and themself and develop these similarities? Or is it preferable to explore the differences between the actor and the character and work on these?

Stanislavski wrote 'An actor must know how to put on and wear a costume ... [he must know] the customs, manners of the times, the ways of greeting people, the use of the fan, sword, cane, hat handkerchief ... He can [only] do all this when he feels himself in his part and his part in himself.'

Clothes have always impacted on human movement. Tight formal clothing restricts, while comfortable and informal clothing frees up movement. Clothing is a primary consideration when a character's physicality is considered. Picture the image of an actor wearing a costume with which he or she, as an individual, is visibly pleased; then compare this image to that of a character who, as represented by the actor, appears and moves in the clothes that 'he' or 'she' has selected. In some present-day costume drama performances it is possible to see modern eyes that lack the innocence of a period; these eyes stare out from faces with an inappropriate day make-up; these characters disport themselves in a manner that demonstrates that the performer (and director) has made no attempt to understand what was norm of socially acceptable behaviour at the time in which the characters are supposed to be living. Does it matter? Throughout the history of acting there have been successful actors who prefer to appear as their recognisable selves what ever role they take on. There have also been actors who set out to explore differences between themselves and the character, and use these to disguise themselves in performance. Where to begin and how? An actor following Stanislavski's System when studying a particular situation which the character faces might ask themself '... if this were real, how would I react? What would I do? ... and normally, naturally ... this *If* acts as a lever to lift him into the world ... of creativity' (*An Actor Prepares*, Constantin Stanislavski, 1936). By comparison Stanislavski's pupil the great actor Michael Chekhov (nephew of the playwright) explained that he endeavoured to capture a character by imitating pictures of its behaviour in his mind's eye: '*I imitated an imaginary character, which itself acted for me in my imagination*' (*The Path of the Actor*, edit. by Andrei Kirillov and Bella Merlin, Routledge, 2005).

Study of the period represented in a play will broaden the actor's knowledge of clothes that people wore in the past. Art galleries offer great opportunities to study fashions of the last centuries. In life, a person selects their clothes based on taste and budget. Each day a person decides what to wear according to the needs of the day. Dressmakers and tailors traditionally have set to out to seduce full wallets and tempt empty heads into spending money in pursuit of the dictates of fashion. Some of the absurdities of eighteenth and nineteenth century fashion styles can still be enjoyed in the caricatures of James Gillray and George Cruikshank. A woman's movement in the days of petticoats and corsets contrasts greatly with the ease of movement possible in today's fashions. Then a young woman would be laced tightly (and painfully) into her corset. In the Hollywood film *Gone with the Wind* actress Vivien Leigh is seen holding on to a bed post while her servant pulls at her corset laces to reduce her already narrow waist size after pregnancy: in extreme cases a woman might have her lower ribs removed to achieve a fashionable body line. Today a young woman lies on her bed as she struggles into her tight jeans to achieve her fashionable body line. The fashionable young man in the past would have expected his tailor to pad the shoulders and breast of his army tunic or morning coat, to enhance his manly out line – a corset was not unknown, tight trousers were not ruled out! The same fashion conscious man in all probability would have been a dangerous opponent when involved in hand to hand fighting, or duelling with sword or pistol; a fine example of expertise with the sword is to be seen in the exceptional duelling action which takes place in the 1952 Hollywood film *Scaramouche* starring Stewart Granger and Mel Ferrer, in which the fighters fence precariously through the precincts of a theatre.

'... You can tell a true artist by his attitude to his costume and properties' (Stanislavski). The actor may find themself wearing dancing pumps, or handmade shoes purchased for show, and dancing in the Assembly Rooms, or promenading in a genteel manner along Bath's North Parade. Shoes and boots can prove challenging for the modern male actor, especially when he experiences the challenges and discomfort of wearing heels.

People who did not have dressmakers and tailors made their own clothes, or accepted clothes that were handed down from employers, or the departed. A former soldier might wear the old trousers that once formed part of his uniform; the sword or musket, that once he had the skill and strength to use in the defence of his country, long gone and his service forgotten. The lady of the manor or vicar's wife might keep a set of baby clothes and blankets to lend to parents, so that a new born baby was kept warm in a poverty-stricken hovel. In their research the actor will find photographs from Victorian times; shocking photographs can be seen of young street children dressed in rags, without shoes and clearly underfed. These photographs from the nineteen century demonstrate the vividly the differences between the 'haves' and the 'have nots' and starkly illustrate existing layers of social status.

Fashion dictates how the fashionable dress their bodies. In the past fashion influenced furniture styles to ensure that people were able to sit down, or that door openings were sufficiently wide to admit a hoop skirt. When fitting costumes the actor will experience how clothes can impact on posture, the performance of physical activities, and on a wearer's mobility and movement. Research will reveal that formerly neither rich nor the poor had access to baths or showers. Deodorants (clothes might be freshened with lavender) and shampoos appeared in the 1860s (rainwater served as a hair conditioner), while dry cleaning was not known.

The actor who wishes to transform themself when representing a character will know that characterisation is not achieved by merely dressing up in a stage costume. Stanislavski wrote 'When you have created even one role, you know how necessary an actor's wig, beard, costume, props, all are to his creation of an image ... Only he who has travelled the difficult path of a achieving a physical form for the character he is to play ... can understand the significance of each detail ... Of make-up and accessories ... A costume or an object appropriate to a stage figure ceases to be a simple material thing, it acquires a kind of sanctity for the actor'.

Period dance and movement

Period dance is taught so the actor can accurately depict the rhythm, music, space, elegance, posture and manners and styles of people and plays written in different times. It works on the universal state in the individual body and with the rest of the group.

Period movement helps with the appropriate deportment for bows, curtseys and gestures of a particular era. It also helps educate the actor in the manners of a period. The actor needs to know that learning the manners of a period should not result in being 'mannered'. The actor learns what was the natural mode of behaviour for that class of person at that time. People in each period took their behaviour for granted, as the normal, natural way; a way of life, not movement. Etiquette was, and still is, a reflection of one's time and status, and expresses the relationship between class and people.

It helps an actor to rehearse in appropriate costume, shoes, and hairstyles, or near enough, to help them transform into the character of the time. An actor just needs to put on a corset or wear tights and a frock coat, a crinoline or a ruff to feel the immediate effect on their physicality. If an actor prepares for an elegant, seventeenth century gentleman or lady in jeans and trainers, they will be giving themselves a lot of extra work to try to marry the text and the physicality. There will be a danger of the appropriate movement being attached later in rehearsal, like an outer garment, rather than being integral to the character and text.

Performing the dances will help the actors become familiar with the strange clothing and to be comfortable with the salutations. Improvising in the period will do the same, although it is best to keep the conversation to a minimum to concentrate on the physicality. Improvisations of character can be played with whilst dancing, once the dances have been learnt.

The dances can be used to research a scene or a play. Romeo and Juliet, or Kate and Petrucchio could dance a Pavane or Alexandreska. Even though they do not dance these dances in a play, a lot can be learnt about the movement and their relationships during the dance, which can be then taken back to the text of the play.

Movement in practice by Madeleine Potter
We were doing *As You Like It* and we were working one day on the scene between Rosalind and Celia (Act 1, sc 2). I found I was unable to communicate something vital having to do with an inner- and outer- grace, a sense of what it means to be noble (the divine right of kings and how that spreads outward to all the court) combined with a sense of being present within an Elizabethan way of being that would free the verse and make it a natural impulse. I was worried that I might make the girls, both very good actresses, self-conscious. It occurred to me that it might be possible to communicate those things in movement, unlocking the unconscious from another direction. I went straight to Jackie at lunch and asked her if she would consider teaching them a dance. She asked me what I needed and immediately said she would teach them a Pavane, a court dance.

Nothing could have prepared us for what happened next. She paired the students off and taught them the dance. She explained about the Elizabethan aesthetic in movement, about how different it is from balletic movement, which came later. Elizabethan dancing is earthy, lower to the ground than ballet, by turns fierce, athletic and almost shockingly graceful. Within half an hour the entire class had moved forward in their thinking and their capacity, empowered by the rhythm and simple majesty of the dance. It was wonderful to see them moving as a whole, and by instinct I asked them each, as they danced, to think of a line of their text, and when I called out their name for them to say it while dancing. It is difficult to describe the power of the result. Jackie and I stood there in amazement as the whole group moved towards us, their lines falling out of them with ease and purpose, as if you were hearing, in the dance, their secrets and desires, like a spy; the psychology of the court. Jackie and I were literally awe-struck by what had been released. It was not only that they were physically inhabiting that world, but also the dance had unlocked the verse, and everyone sounded as if they were speaking the way they had always spoken, words they had come up with just that moment. It was natural and utterly focused. They were individually, and collectively, free.

Jackie and I have continued to use that exercise. I often begin my Shakespeare scene presentations with it, as it is a very good way to connect the actor to their own part, and the group as a whole connects, as an observer once said, dreaming the same dream. The hypnotic effect of the Pavane and iambic verse has been noticed by all sorts of audiences; Jackie and I have both done it outside of BADA (notably in a Shakespeare workshop in HMP Brixton). Its simple and effective design simply never fails to illuminate not only the text, but the particular acting dynamic of a specific group.

Two years ago I did *Present Laughter*, and in the same way as with the Shakespeare, I was trying to convey a sense of the 1920s that cannot be communicated by words. Jackie created an exercise that put them in a daydream of a typical day of a socialite in the roaring twenties. The specificity of the detail was amazing to me, the bath, the marble floor, the cocktail, the silk stockings. It is not an exaggeration to say that afterwards everyone looked and moved differently. And as before, Coward's lines came out of them with ease and the authority of understanding.

18 Period dance

An overview of period dance by Michael Gaunt

People have always danced and dance has many forms. Over time mankind has danced to express spirituality, joy and moments of celebration and, importantly, dance has been a medium for social interaction between men and women. In the West, dance, as with the theatre and other pleasurable human pursuits, at various times in history been condemned by authority for being sinful. Happily, in the West those censorious days are past and today dance in all its forms is freely experienced and enjoyed by audiences and every kind of dancer.

Young men and women have always been drawn to dance and dancing, not least because it brought them in contact with each other for the same lovely reasons that have been enjoyed since the beginning of mankind. In the past, society's rules made it difficult for the young to meet members of the opposite sex and opportunities to do so usually had to be taken at family, or family-approved social occasions. These strictures on behaviour were regularly introduced into plays and scripts throughout the centuries: actors will be aware of them in the plays of the Elizabethan and Restoration periods. They are also to be found in the eighteenth and nineteenth centuries' comedy of manners and melodramas: playwrights were able to introduce a lot of fun by allowing young lovers to thwart the wishes of their parents and guardians. Audiences still enjoy the conventions, manners and romance of past times in stories, old and new, which make up the present diet of television and film costume dramas. In the past it was not easy for young people to arrange to meet. They contrived to make this happen by attending theatre performances, if this were permitted, or could be done in secret; or, by visiting lending libraries, where there was the added advantage of being able to borrow the latest sensational novels; this was the habit of Lydia Languish heroine of Sheridan's *The Rivals*: Lydia was in love with the thought of being in love! If permitted, a visit to the houses of friends with attractive brothers or sisters was another ploy. Failing this, as a final resort, there might be an opportunity to glimpse the adored one on a Sunday across the pews in church. Greater opportunities were permitted at a formal ball in a town's assembly rooms, the hunt ball, and the town and country house balls. Such events provided young men and women with a legitimate chance to meet and view each other more openly, while at the same time ambitious mothers might use these occasions to target landed and rich, eligible, young (usually, but not always) men to marry their daughters. And so throughout the seventeenth, eighteenth, nineteenth and twentieth centuries the young have been ever grateful to musicians who ceaselessly played the Farandole, the Galliard, the Pavane and the ensuing dance styles that followed through to the arrival of the waltz. Strict etiquette was followed at a ball, and young women carried dance cards on which young men sought to have their names written against a particular dance: at this stage the ladies were in charge, as long as their mothers approved the names on the list. Lady Bracknell's interview with John Worthing in Wildes's *The Importance of Being Earnest* provides a useful and humorous guide to the questions an aristocratic mother might have put to a prospective bridegroom. The film of the play provides a unique opportunity to observe a cast of actors who really understood and empathised with the characters, timing and the intrinsic style of this late nineteenth century comedy. The film is finely directed, designed, cast and is true to the original text.

Actors can speculate about what the dancers might have chit-chatted to each other as they glided and turned to the music; or guess at what nervous lovers whispered to each other as they whirled around a fine room and became intoxicated by each other's nearness. Informal country dancing in villages provided similar opportunities for the lower echelon of society and here the dancing and atmosphere would no doubt have been generally much freer than in a country house. Thus dancing provided unique opportunities for men and women from all levels of society to meet in close proximity. In polite society there were formalities to be observed and these dictated how a male approached a female when requesting permission to dance, or how at the end of the dance she was escorted back to her party, and how she in turn responded. In the past it was not permitted to hold one's partner when dancing and choreography ensured that touching was limited: touching came later when the waltz arrived from Vienna and scandalised polite society: for a while. Young women traditionally were chaperoned, which also limited opportunities for meeting the opposite sex. When a young women eventually danced with the one she loved, or thought she loved, she was sometimes literally swept off her feet: the meeting of eyes, touching of hands, waists and shoulders could be intoxicating, if they belonged to the right person.

Following the appalling experience of the First World War social formalities began to ease as jazz and popular music exerted their warming influence and young people began to find their freedom and independence. It became easier to meet and mix with the opposite sex, although the chaperone did not immediately disappear. By the time the Second World War ended, it can be noticed that dance partners had got closer to each other; and when they danced the jive they became surprisingly athletic with few holds barred. At the same time in the dance halls when the slow last waltz was played at the evening's end, it could be noticed that the dancers danced very, very close and they were not judged. Ironically, once the freedom to dance closely had been achieved it became less important and today couples in night clubs can be seen dancing quite separately and doing their own thing!

Typically in a straight play, or film script, dance may be interpolated within the action to illustrate a period of time, its codes of behaviour, atmosphere, and how characters were permitted to relate to one another. In a musical the 'triple threat' of acting, singing and dancing is used to inject levels of energy and vitality to illustrate the time frame, period manners, relationships and to advance a book's narrative: the character, not only acts, but sings and dances out its story.

There are numerous dances for each period and I have chosen a select few which help to establish and develop the skills needed in observation, transformation and achieving the universal state. Moreover, the dances can be used to refine the students' research skills. Whilst the dances I have chosen have been explained in historical order, they can be taught out of sequence to complement other aspects of the students' training, such as plays and projects they are working on. At the end of this chapter there is a glossary of the period dance terms to describe the following terms.

⊙ **Teaching point** (DVD: Exercise 32)

There is far more to teaching the dances than just the steps, so the classes need careful planning to incorporate plenty of movement work which then branches into this work. The dances themselves do, however, in their pure form, teach the actor about posture, space, movement and rhythm.

Medieval dance

For each of the dances explained below, it is essential that the student is given the opportunity to research the historical context, including political and social systems, main events, costume, architecture, art and religion.

To appreciate a simple objective of pre-16th century social dances it is useful to understand something of the beliefs of the medieval world. As Belinda Quirey mentions in her book, *May I Have the Pleasure*, sympathetic magic was at the heart of the dances at this time, where man saw himself as using his energy in a compatible way to assist the forces of nature. The Medieval cosmological viewpoint was of a geocentric universe: the earth stood motionless with the sun, moon and planets orbiting around it marking an observable east to west journey across the sky. The shadow cast by the sun on a stick in the ground moves in a clockwise direction throughout the day, so to keep in harmony with the planets and join the forces of nature, pre-16th century dances set off with the left foot and moved clockwise.

The Carole

This is a chain dance and has two different forms. One is circular, the second linear. The nature of these dances provide an ideal opportunity for the teacher and student to concentrate on the universal posture, walking practice, leading and following, working as an ensemble. It also allows the student to explore the use of space and rhythm. In the medieval carole dances, the time signature is not what really counts, they can be in simple or compound time.

According to the *ISTD Medieval Anthology* (ed. Terry Worroll), 'Linear carole: almost any tune that can sustain a fairly brisk walking tempo could be [used] in compound time to help keep the flow and "soften" the accents of the regular beats. Christmas carols such as *In Dulci Jubilo* or *I Saw Three Ships* and so on make welcome additions. Circular carole: similarly, almost any eight bar phrase will suffice for the branle double and branle gai and any six bar melody for the branle simple. Carols could also be used'.

Branles – circle dance

The word branler means to sway in old French, but it means that the whole circle is swaying, not the bodies. Set off on the left foot in a clockwise circular direction and the swaying motion will push the circle further clockwise than anti-clockwise.

The suite of branles

Branles double (8 bar phrase or units of 8 beats)

1. Hold hands in a circle. The circle can be open or closed. An open circle is one with an opening of two people.
2. Start with feet together.
3. On the left foot, take four walks to the left i.e. left, right, left then close the right foot to the left. Repeat to the right on the right foot.

Teaching point

In order that the circle moves more clockwise than anti-clockwise, the steps need to be larger to the left than to the right.

Branles Simples (6 bar phrases or units of 6 beats)

1. Take four walks to the left, starting on the left, i.e. left, right, left, then bring the right foot to close.
2. Turn to the right.
3. Step the right foot to the right and bring the left foot to close.

Branles Gai (6/8 time)

1. Everyone in the circle turns to the left, bend the right leg as you simultaneously slide the left leg out in front of you, body upright.
2. Spring from foot to foot, left, right, left, and finally back on the right sliding the left through for the final two counts.
3. Repeat 8 times.

Branles de Borgone (duple time)

1. Everyone stands with their bodies turned to the left, feet parallel.
2. Set off on the left foot: left, right, left and hop on the left foot as you swing the right leg with bent knee.
3. Moving the body in the same direction, repeat the action on the other side: right foot, left foot, right foot and hop on to the right foot. Then, swing on the left foot with bent knee.

The Farandole – line dance

This can be danced to any music that is at walking speed. Tunes in 6/8 or compound time are good because they kep the flow. The farandole is the earliest known western European dance and is excellent for walking practice, group or team work, spatial patterns, basic walking rhythm and learning the art of leading a group and being led. It is made up of 'figures' or floor patterns and the steps are very simple, including walking, skipping and running.

The dance is not gender-specific and can be executed with any number of people and it can be done in two groups.

The figures
The serpentine
1. The group hold hands in a long line, with the leader's left hand leading the dance.
2. The line sets off at walking pace, in time with the music.
3. The dance makes a snake-like floor pattern, all over the space.
4. If there are two groups then the leader's job is to make sure that the lines both balance the space with each other. This means that they need to work the shape of their lines to be in sympathy with one another.

Teaching point

Make sure that the leader is taking care of the rest of the group from an acting perspective. That is just calmly leading the group in a safe way giving confidence through the body. The rest of the line has an easy hand hold with free shoulders and un-stiff arms. Strong free arm and leg swings are a good preparation for this dance, the arm swing for an easy hand hold and the leg swing for an easy walk.

Thread the needle
This is the only figure which changes the leader.

1. As the line is being lead in a snake-like shape around the space, the leader curves round, to the second person and stands directly in front of them. Simultaneously they swing their right arm up to make an arch between them and the second person.
2. The second person then lets go of the third person's hand and leads the third person through the arch with their right hand. The rest of the line follows through and when the last person goes through, they take the leader's left hand and pulls them through the arch.
3. Now the new leader is the previous third person.

L'Escargot or The snail
1. The leader starts at the tail and winds the line in to a tight snail like shape, until they meet the second person.
2. They then swing their right arm back, sends the second person back and round and then walks forward.
3. The first and second person walk along, side by side, as the rest of the line winds its way under and finally out the other side.

Teaching points

To make this work the leader must bring the line round as if they are going to make a big circle and then instead of joining hands with the end person, they then carry on past them, looking at them and then the next person, etc. This keeps the spiral tight so that when they finally reach the person next to them, the rest of the line is wound up in a tight spiral and allows the line to uncurl successfully.

Before attempting this, it's a good idea to get the students in a line. Break the line in twos starting from the far left. Then each person practices, swinging their partner round and back. This enables everybody to have a go at that unnatural movement without having the rest of the line to contend with and get all tangled up.

The arches

1. The leader waits until all the line can see them, then they stand still, next to the second person. They then take their right arm up into the air, and the rest of the group does the same. This makes a whole line of arches.
2. The leader then sets off weaving in and out of all the arches, starting by going under the second and third person. They keep on weaving until they get to the other end, then takes the line carefully on back into the serpentine figure.

Teaching points

There are two movements in this figure, depending where you are standing in the arches. Before you start tackling the whole line, split the lines into five or sixes and then practice with this amount of people. Keep changing the leader until everybody has had a chance to lead. The key to successful arches is to keep the arms and shoulders free and the hands loose for slipping round.

Then the next tip is to wait to be tugged by the shoulder and follow the tug. Sometimes it will pull you forward and through and another time it will pull you backwards. Either way, you need to keep the arms up above your head and keep the arches high, until you are under then you let them drop down.

Linear hey

The linear hey or grand chain can only be done if there are two lines.

1. The leaders set up the hey by dancing the serpentine and balancing the space with each other, when the two groups are in diagonally opposite corners of the room.
2. Then walk toward each other and take left hands, curving through the line take hands alternately with the rest of the line. When the leaders come out of the other end they then carry on walking until the rest of their line catch up with them and then they carry on dancing the serpentine , the escargot, the arches and the thread the needle.

> **Teaching point**
> *To teach a hey first begin with the circular hey, to enable the students to understand the concept of taking hands on the first note and looking each other in the eye. When they have mastered this, then move on to the linear hey, where there is the added complication of coming out of it at the end. Use a 3/4 rhythm.*
>
> 1. *The actors stand in a circle and hold hands.*
> 2. *Turn and face their partner.*
> 3. *Everybody walk forward on the left foot and take right hands with their partner on the count of one.*
> 4. *Carry on walking in a curve around the right shoulder, right foot then left foot, still holding right hands. (Counts two and three.)*
> 5. *Then take left hands with the next person on the count of one, left hand with the right foot following it through with two more steps (left and right) repeat all the way around the circle.*

The Italian Renaissance

Bassa Danza

This is a composed dance with a triple rhythm. Often it is a couple dance but can also be done with three people. Each dance has a title of its own and steps are performed close to the floor. Sometimes, for variety and a bit fun of, the more elevated Saltarello was introduced into the dance, but never to such an extent that it spoiled the general serenity of the dance.

The following dances are used in actor training to develop the use of space, rhythm and relationships, along with the transformation of the physicality.

Alexandreska

This is a court dance, done in 3/4 time. Unlike the other dances above, it uses the whole floor, the relationship is with just one person; the steps and body movement are more complex. Two people would dance the whole dance while the rest of the courtiers would watch and then another couple would get up and dance. The exacting nature of this dance improves physical technique and projection whilst at the same time teaching the students to hold relationships across a large space.

The teacher needs to be aware that there needs to be a strong focus on posture, alignment and balance in relation to the body, relationships and space.

1. The couple start at the back centre of the room. The man stands in front of the lady both facing The Presence. Imagine two tram lines going down the centre of the room.

Figures and steps

1st figure: the man leads the lady into the dance.

Steps: simple left, simple right, double left (using maniera).

At this point the men and women do different steps.

Men: crossed simple, taking the right foot over the left and ending up facing the back of the room on the second imaginary tram line (counts 1, 2).

Double towards the back, starting on the left foot (counts 1, 2, 3 and 4).

Crossed simple right foot over left to face the front, ending up on the first tram line (counts 1, 2).

The men end up behind the woman.

Women: simple forward on the right foot (counts 1, 2).

Double on the left, travelling over to the other tram line, following the man towards the back wall.

Crossed simple right foot over left, ending up on the first tram line (count 1, 2).

2. Both perform a Continenza and a Reverence to the courtiers and The Presence.
3. This sequence is repeated with the man and lady performing the opposite roles followed by a Continenza and a Reverence to the courtiers and The Presence.

2nd figure − figure of eight

1. The lady shadows the man's floor pattern as they both do these steps which make a figure of eight:
   - Simple left, simple right, double left, simple right, simple left, double right.

3rd figure − S shape

1. At the end of the figure of eight the couple are in the centre of the room.
2. The lady makes the top half of the S shape by turning to her right, heading to the back of the room, carving the top of the S shape as she moves.
3. Simultaneously the man moves to the bottom of the room making the bottom half of the S shape.
4. During this floor pattern both man and lady will be doing double on the left and double on the right and will end up facing each other on the diagonal and finish with a Continenza and Reverence to each other.

4th figure − spiral

1. Performing seven passing simples, finishing closing the right leg to the left.
2. Starting on the outer circle moving to the inner circle the lady will finish on the man's right, thereby making a spiral shape on the floor.
3. The man and woman link their little fingers with their hands at shoulder height.
4. Then they both perform simple left, simple right and do a Reverence to the Presence staying down on their left knees.

Venus

Venus has two rhythms: duple and triple. Duple for the opening of the dance and then triple from the first set of pivas.

This rendition of Venus is based on that of Mabel Dolmetsch's version of the dance. This is a very beautiful Italian Renaissance dance, for three people. Owing to the pureness of the dance, once the challenging steps are mastered, the student is able to explore the multitude of relationships which emerge from the trio.

1. Three people stand next to each other at the top of the room in the centre, usually with a man in the middle and a woman on either side; but it can also be done with three women, three men or a woman in the middle and a man on either side. Each combination will change the emphasis on the relationships.
2. The person in the middle is A and the people on the outside are B. The person on A's right is B1 and the person on A's left is B2.

First section

1. The first step is called movimento (see glossary) A and Bs all step to the left, close the feet and then rise and sink; using maniera.
2. A and Bs do simple left and simple right (in line with one another).
3. Then A does a repraisa (stepping back on the left foot diagonal back and gesturing to B1).
4. He then does a repraisa back on the right foot to right diagonal back gesturing to B2, while simultaneously B1 and B2 do two doubles with maniera on the sprung foot, going straight forward to the front of the room toward The Presence.
5. A performs a volta tonda i.e. crossed simple right foot over left foot (counts 1, 2 to face the left wall). Open simple on the left foot, moving up to the back wall 3, 4, and a crossed repraisa right foot over left foot (5, 6, 7, close right foot to left foot).
6. Simultaneously the Bs are performing crossed reprais; left foot over right foot, closing the right foot to the left foot (1, 2, 3, 4) to face the back and then repraisa to the right (5, 6, 7, 8).
7. A and B move towards each other, performing a double on the left foot with maniera (1, 2, 3, 4).
8. Then A steps to the left and bows to B1 and then to the right and bows to B2 at the same time as B1 and B2 go down on one knee in a Renaissance bow, angling in on the diagonal to A.

Second section (6/8 or 2/4)

1. A takes B1's right hand and they both perform four pivas around each other (i.e. up, up, down, 1 and a 2 and a 3 and a 4).
2. Then A takes B2's left hand and performs four pivas around B, interrupting the final count to do a maniera in a line of three (5 and a 6 and 7 and a maniera 8).
3. Everybody links little fingers in a line in the centre of the room.
4. All do simple left, simple right (still linking) and then A pulls the two Bs around to face them (1, 2) while the Bs step on their inside leg with the other leg behind and then bow down on one knee to A and stay on one knee.

Third section

1. A sets off down the room toward The Presence performing four pivas starting on the left foot (up, up, down, 1 and a 2 and a 3 and a 4) leaving the left foot extended in front and cross left foot over right foot in a simple, then a simple with the left foot to the left (1, 2).

2. Meanwhile B1 and B2 come up from the bow, pressing down on the front leg, leaving the back leg behind for four counts (up 2, 3, 4).

3. Then crossed simple, right over left (1, 2) and open simple to the right (3, 4).

4. Both A and B1 and B2 perform two saltarello. The Bs coming down the room and A going up the room (up, down, up, down, step spring, and up, down, up, down, step spring).

5. End the last spring with the left leg extended in front and cross it over the right leg in a simple and taking the left leg back, go down on the left knee in a bow.

6. A now does a final volta tonda interrupting the end with a maniera and holding little fingers with B1 on their right and B2 on their left.

7. B simultaneously performs seven pivas travelling up the space in a big arc ending next to A on either side and on the eight count performing a maniera altogether.

8. All link little fingers perform a simple to the left and a simple to the right and go down on the left knee in a bow.

High Renaissance France and Elizabethan England

Sellenger's round

This dance is an Elizabethan country dance, in 6/8 time, based on a mediaeval round dance. It would have been danced around a stone or a tree. The whole class make male and female couples with the lady on the man's right. All the couples join hands and make a big circle.

Teaching point

The dance is divided into introductions and choruses. The chorus repeats all the way through the dance and the introduction changes.

First introduction

1. Taking eight counts, walk to the left: left, right, left, right, left right, left and bring your right foot to the left foot. Repeat anti-clockwise setting off on the right foot.

The chorus

1. Moving into the circle, simple left, simple right, moving back a double on the right foot, closing feet together to turn and face your partner.

2. Facing your partner, simple left, simple right, double round your left shoulder.

3. Finish facing the centre.

4. Repeat.

Second introduction

1. Face the centre and drop hands.
2. Move forward a double on the left foot, back a double on the right foot.
3. Repeat.

Second chorus (as above)

Third introduction – siding

1. Passing by one another's right shoulder (with your partner in a curved shape), double step on your left foot, and double step back on your right foot.
2. Repeat.

Third chorus (as above)

Fourth introduction – arming

1. Take the right arm with your partner, making a full circle, setting off on the left foot: left, right, left, right, left, right, left and bring your right foot to the left foot on the count of eight.
2. Repeat to the right, setting off on the right foot and taking the left arm.

Fourth chorus (as above)

Fifth introduction

1. Fifteen walks to the left, starting on the left and finishing bringing the right leg to the left finishing on sixteen counts.

'...Why dost thou not go to church in a galliard and come home in a coranto? My very walk should be a jig; I would not so much as make water but in a sink-a-pace.'

TWELFTH NIGHT, ACT 1, SCENE III

☺ The Galliard (DVD: Exercise 33)

This is man's solo, in 6/4 or 3/4 time. It is very athletic and exuberant and can be improvised on the rhythm. There is a story which said that Queen Elizabeth would have danced it thirty two times in the morning before breakfast for her exercise! Also, that she often picked her courtiers on whether they could dance a good Galliard. It would mean they were fit with a bright mind! It is energetic and requires neat footwork, and was performed bare-headed, hat in hand. Men danced it athletically with elegance.

The rhythm of the Galliard is 1, 2, 3, 4, 5, and 6. Think of the tune God Save our Gracious Queen as the rhythm for the Galliard. The 'and' is very important, as it forms the cadence at the end of the leap after you have been in the air for some of count 4 and all of count 5, after which you drop on to the landing foot on 'and', and touch the toe forward without weight, on count 6.

Stand with the feet parallel.

Counts

1. Jump onto the left foot, bending the left knee as you extend the right leg out in front of you, keeping the legs parallel.
2. Swing the right leg behind as you hop on the left leg, legs parallel.
3. Cut the right leg into the left leg, driving the left leg forward as you spring onto the right leg.
4. Spring changing legs, keeping the legs in front and in parallel (you are now on the left leg with the right leg stretched out in front).
4.5 Hop high into the air, on the left leg.
5 Stay in the air.
And 6 Cadenza, changing legs, landing on the right foot and placing down the left foot on the ground lightly in front.

The arms swing in opposition with the front leg and then on the Cadenza make a small circle with the hands and landing with the hands as if on two drums below the hips.

Repeat the whole five step on the other side, the tricky bit being making sure you lift the right leg up in the air as you hop on the first count.

The Fighting Cock

This is the same rhythm as before.

Counts

1. Draw the right leg up onto the left shin, turned out, as the left leg is stretched and you go up onto the toe (releve), while the arms turn in towards each other and stretch down toward the straight leg and the head turns to the right over the bent leg.
2. Place the right foot behind the left foot and bend the knees (while the arms come in front like cockerel claws).
3. Draw the left leg up the shin and rise on the right leg, stretching it (releve, while the arms and head are as number 1).
4. Place the left foot behind the right foot while you simultaneously stretch the right foot in front on a swish and on a bent left knee while the arms are as number 2).
4.5 Hop up into the air.
5. Stay in the air
And 6. Cadenza.

The Scottish Step

1. Leap over onto the right leg, while the left foot plants the heel against the right ankle in front (as in a Coup de Pied in ballet). While the arms are above the head with the pointing finger and thumb are together (like fifth position in ballet).
2. Hop on the right foot, planting the left foot coupe de pied behind, keeping the arms above the head in fifth position.

3. Swish the left foot behind keeping it in the air, in parallel, as you hop on the right foot, keeping the arms above the head.
4. Cut the left foot into the right foot, sending the right foot forward straight in front keeping the arms above the head.
4.5 Hop into the air.
5. Stay in the air.
And 6. Cadenza.

The Pacing Step

1. Set off on the left leg, to the left, and walk in time to the Galliard rhythm, i.e.
step left, 1, 2, step right, across left, 3, 4, step left, leaving the right leg extended out to the side and turn 5 and 6.
2. Repeat to the right.
3. Repeat to the left.
4. Repeat to the right.
6. As you are pacing, keep the head facing the front and make a figure of eight shape with the arms as if you are flourishing a big cloak in front of your body. The pacing should have a Spanish feel to it.

To dance the Galliard, do a big bow on the Galliard rhythm then do:

- Four Five Steps.
- Four Pacing.
- Four Fighting Cocks.
- Four Pacing.
- Four Scottish Steps.
- Four Pacing.
- Bow.

Example

Henry V (by William Shakespeare, directed by Richard Olivier, Shakespeare's Globe, London, 1997). As the play had an all male cast, I had to help the men to act as women. This took technical, physical precision as well as physical transformation. There was the added complication of the actors needing female Elizabethan deportment simultaneously. At the end of the production there was a jig, which was with the full cast to the rhythm of the Galliard. At one point there was a break in the jig when three men came out and danced a pure Galliard. This in turn was interrupted by three men acting as women, who danced the female version of the Galliard. By learning this dance the actors were able to inhabit the rhythm and world of the play at a much deeper level and the discipline, rigour and muscularity that the dance requires enabled them to fully immerse themselves into the physical life of sixteenth century people.

The Pavane

This is a sedate and dignified couple dance, similar to the 15th century bassadanza, in 4/4 time, which according to Belinda Quirey, was 'Baffling in its simplicity'. These can be done as a couple dance, or as a procession.

The lady is on the man's right holding hands low and when he bows then she does a curtsey.

1. Bow and curtsey, making sure the man and lady half bow toward each other and half out to the front (men step back on the left foot and bend the left knee, while the front leg is extend out in front, and the lady keep both heels together, feet slightly turned out and bend the knees all the way down to the floor and stretch them).

Counts:

1, 2, 3, 4	and a curtsey and bow: down, down, down, up and a
1, 2,	simple to the left (step on to the ball of the foot and sink down on the heels, feet together)
3, 4,	simple to the right (technique as above).
5, 6, 7, 8,	double forward stepping up on to the ball the left foot (left, right, left sink heels down to the floor i.e. up, up, up, down).
1, 2,	simple right.
3,4	simple
5, 6, 7, 8	double back setting off on the right foot (right, left, right sink heels into the floor, with feet together).

Repeat until the music ends.

As a procession

○ The couples are lined up behind each other in a long snake round the room.
○ As the lady is on the outside the man has to make sure his steps are not too long, so the lady does not get left behind on the outer curve of the circle.
○ The procession can go all around the room, finishing by coming down the room to The Presence.

The Coranto

This is in 12/8 time.

1. All hold hands in a Farandole line.
2. Everybody does a Coranto Simple on the left leg, a Coranto Simple on the right leg, and a Coranto Double on the left leg.
3. Repeat this starting on the right leg.

The Elizabethan version is jumped and skipped, whereas later, in the restoration period, it became the Courante, and was a simple version of the minuet.

Seventeenth century or Restoration dance

Baroque dance dates roughly from 1600–1750, and is closely linked with Baroque music, theatre and opera. The dances of this time included English country dance and the French Noble style. Most dance in the 17th and 18th centuries originated at the French court of Louis XIV, and it is here that we see the first clear stylistic ancestor of classical ballet. It is often referred to casually as baroque dance in spite of the existence of other theatrical and social dance styles during the baroque era.

The Minuet

The minuet comes from France and is an elegant dance which has three even beats. The minute became one of a special set of dances called the Dance Suite.

People would dance differently depending on where they were, who they were, who was watching and also how much alcohol they had drunk. In a tavern, dancing would be unconventional and free; in a ballroom, it would be refined and graceful. This can be fully explored by the student, once they have mastered the complicated and balletic steps along with flourishing arm movements.

The minuet is danced by one couple alone, while the rest of the courtiers look on. It has a fixed sequence of figures: lead-in, right-hand turn, left-hand turn, and two-hand turn closing. These are punctuated by a Z figure. While the sequence of figures is fixed, dancers can vary the spacing and number of hand turns by interrupting them with Z figures. The number of minuet steps used in each figure depends on the length of the tune and the size of the dancing space.

The dance is made up of the minuet steps while dancing the figures. The steps and figures are described, separately, below.

The minuet steps

Minuet steps are in 3/4 time. The basic minuet step combination consists of four steps in six beats (two measures) of music.

1. Begin with a plié (a bend of the legs) on the left foot flat, then on up-beat .
2. Rise to the ball of the right foot on beat 1, straightening both legs, heels close together.
3. Plié on the right foot flat on beat 2.
4. Rise to the ball of the left foot on beat 3, straightening both legs, heels close together.
5. Keeping legs straight, walk forward on the ball of the right, then left foot on beats 4 and 5 (or 1 and 2 of second measure of music).
6. On beat 6, sink into plié on left foot flat.
7. Start again on beat one, rising to the ball of the right foot.

Figures

Partners face each other in the centre of the floor. The dance begins with a bow and curtsey to the audience and a bow and curtsey to their partner. This is called the honours.

Lead-in figure: dance curving sideways to meet at back of space, then forward to middle, holding inside hands. Man wheels partner around 3/4, then both dance sideways to corner of space.

Z figure: dance sideways to other corner, then cross diagonally through middle of space, changing corners, then sideways to each other's previous corner.

Right-hand turn: from the corner, dance sideways to the other corner, then diagonally to meet, taking right hands. Turn by right hand, then dance sideways back to the corner.

Z figure: (once or twice).

Left-hand turn: as right-hand turn, but with left.

Z figure: (once or twice)

Two-hand turn and ending: from the corner, dance sideways to the other corner, then forward to meet. Take two hands and turn. Keeping hands, dance sideways to the back of the space, opening out to face audience at the end.

Honour the audience, then the partner.

Minuet steps are in 3/4 time. The basic minuet step-combination consists of four steps in six beats (two measures) of music.

How to use dance as physical research for a play

The actor when researching a character in a specific period of time can choose to consolidate their preparation by identifying what was special or different in the way that people conducted their everyday lives. Visiting a house of the period and walking through its rooms and soaking up its atmosphere can set the imagination working. The shallow stair risers of a grand staircase that enabled long-gowned ladies to glide effortlessly up and down and in and out of the rooms of a house contrast markedly with those of a modern staircase. Ham House in Surrey, built in 1610, is a rewarding place to visit, as it is a house where generations of privileged men and women have lived throughout the centuries. What have these elegant and well-proportioned rooms witnessed? The house has no electric light and becomes atmospherically interesting on a winter's day as the natural light fades and the shadows deepen. At the other end of the social scale is John Shakespeare's house, the birthplace of William, in Stratford upon Avon. The accommodation reflects the simple standard of a family living in a working household. It is a special place in which to let the imagination run as the various rooms are explored; what words were spoken in them? What did people living in this house know which we can never know? What do we know that they could never have known? What did they talk about? What did Shakespeare experience in that little town and how was he drawn to the theatre?

While dance can be used as a means to set up ambience and relationships within a play, its presence does not always lead to a happy ending. Two plays can be considered in which dance initially triggers the narrative and brings men and women close together, in one case for love, and in the other out of lust, and this closeness in both instances leads to tragic death. In the fifth scene of Act One of *Romeo and Juliet* Capulet, Juliet's father, enters with his family and guests and calls out '… Come, musicians, play. A hall, a hall, give room! and foot it girls'. Romeo first sees Juliet when she is dancing in her father's house surrounded by kinsmen who are literally his deadly enemies. He contrives to dance with her and in that moment he loves her and she loves him back: the audience sees them dancing in those first minutes when they become lost in each other. They experience a profound life-changing (and ending) moment: he wants her as his wife, his objective is to win her and she responds, she wants him as her husband. Building on that first meeting and the memory of the dance, the actors playing the lovers will seek to find actions and moments with which to represent the lovers' emotions and deepening love for each other; a love that faces obstacles, obstacles that finally cannot be overcome and death is the outcome.

Strinberg's naturalistic play *Miss Julie* written in 1888 was influenced by his difficult relationships with women and his interest in psychology. The action takes place on an estate that belongs to Miss Julie's father who is a count. At the opening of the play we learn about Miss Julie's broken engagement. Her father's servant, Jean, is heard saying 'Miss Julie is mad again tonight absolutely mad ... she asked me to be her partner in the waltz and ... from that moment she danced in such a way I have never seen'. Miss Julie then enters in a state of physical elation following her energised dancing, which she wishes to continue and she instructs Jean to take her arm and saying 'Don't talk of orders, this evening we lay aside rank. Give me your arm'. Miss Julie has joined in the midsummer day celebrations on her father's estate and has danced freely with her father's employees. The audience does not witness this dancing but sees her subsequent high spirits. The wine has flowed, the atmosphere is heady and excitement is in the air. Miss Julie has spent the evening flirting with Jean: a high status woman playing with a low status man. Jean is self-educated, travelled and ambitious. They are attracted to each other and the flirting leads them to sudden sexual intercourse and in the heat of the moment they plan to run away. At this moment they exchange their status levels – he becomes powerful and she dependant. They lose their courage and are unable to leave the estate. She asks him what is to be done and he hands her his razor. The play ends as she leaves the room razor in hand.

In conclusion, a brief word on the role of dance in an actor's training. In his book *Building a Character* (Stanislavski), Stanislavski wrote the following '... [The dance] is not part of ... body work. Its role ... is contributory, preparing us for other important exercises ... It is an excellent corrective for the position of arms, legs, backs ... Ballet exercises at the barre are ... splendid. Of equal importance for plasticity and expressiveness of the body is the development of the extremities of the arms and legs, the wrists, fingers, ankles. Learn [from your dancing lessons] to acquire ways of developing, reinforcing and placing your vertebrae ... Whereas gymnastics develop motions that are clear cut to the point of abruptness ... dancing tends to produce fluency, breadth, cadence in gesture'.

Glossary of period dance terms

Cadenza (count: and 8): this is where the left leg is bent and then the right leg is swept in front as you hop into the air off the left leg and land on the right leg and place the left toe down on to the floor.

Coranto Doubles: jump up of both feet and skip forward onto the left foot, right foot, left foot and land feet together (and-a-one, and-a-two, and-a-three, and-a-four).

Coranto Simples: start with the feet together and jump up off both feet and split the legs on the way down landing on the right foot and sending the left foot forward and skip landing both feet together (count: and-a-one and-a two).

Crossed Simple: this takes takes two beats. Cross the right leg over the left and bring the left foot into to close against the right foot whilst simultaneously turning a quarter of a turn.

Doubles: these take four beats. As with the simples, they too can be done on a raised or flat foot. Step forward onto the left foot. Step on the right foot (as if walking past) then on the left foot and close the right foot to the left foot.

Maniera: this is a full body movement in which the head and spine turn towards the working leg, and the arms work in the same direction as the body. Often the simples and doubles are danced with maniera.

Movimento: stand with feet together. Take a step to the left and whilst closing the right, then perform a maniera with the body and rise and sink with the feet.

Open Simples: a simple takes two beats. It can be executed forward, backwards or to the side. It can be done on the flat foot or on the sprung foot.

Passing Simples: step onto the ball of the left foot, out to the side. Cross the right leg over the left, and bend the knee, keeping the feet turned out and the hips square to the front.

Pivas (3 counts: up, up, down): step up onto the left foot on a sprung foot (see p. 30). Step past on the right foot (sprung foot) and step through on the left foot on a flat foot and knee bent.

The Presence: this is the person who sits at the top of the room and is the most important person in the room, for example, the king, the queen or the person whose party it is.

Repraisa: this is the same movement as a simple except that it done to four counts. It needs a lot of strength in the legs to balance and draw the second leg smoothly to the first. It can be executed open, crossed and turning.

Saltarelli (6 counts: up, down, up, down, step spring): step on to the ball of the left foot, step down onto the right foot with a bent leg, step up onto the ball of the left foot again and down onto the right step through onto the left foot and spring (like a little hitch kick in front).

Siding: a term in country dance when the couple move toward each other, shoulder to shoulder, or moves around each other for example, to move forward a double and siding means walk forward left foot, right foot, left foot and close right foot to left (4 counts) and shoulder to shoulder with your partner.

Simples: step forward on the left foot (and 1). Bring the right foot to join it to the left foot, (and 2).

Volta tonda: this is a turn made up of a crossed simple (1, 2), an open simple (3, 4) and a crossed repraisa (5, 6, 7, 8).

Movement in practice

The Man of Mode, director: Matthew Smith

Rehearsals began with pure movement into period movement to bring the cast together into the physical world of the play.

The movement work included walking on curves, sitting and standing, bows and curtseys and fans and canes, for the whole cast and then each individual used the researach to develop their own individual physical character.

Seventeenth century English country dance was used as further research into the rhythm and style of the play and then finally an English country dance was choreographed for during the play and also to finish the play, blending with the curtain call.

Conclusion
by Robert Price

To work on your voice: work on your body

The reason why I started going to the theatre as a young man was for a chance to look at people – for permission. For the theatre is perhaps above all an essentially physical place; a very bodied and blooded place. A very un-Facebook kind of a place. In our real lives, unless we're playing with other people in the closest of intimacies (our lovers, our children) we tend only to glance at bodies. We try to ignore them; or if we do receive the information and emotion communicated through our bodily tensions and shapes, we receive it unconsciously. Or we might sit in a cafe window or on the top of a bus to allow ourselves the full pleasure and diversion of watching others through the agreed contract of public places: that we can gaze, so long as we are furtive. So we're allowed to look sometimes, but we mustn't be seen to be looking by the person we're looking at.

In the theatre though, we can look and look and look – at a whole person, from top to tail. We can stare. And we're allowed to. And we also get to watch bodies move out of stillness into action and behaviour. So in a playhouse we get to watch a whole person in grief, we get to watch whole bodies arguing or flirting. We see that people are so much more than their faces and as we watch the drama we learn to understand that in a theatre these bodies and the way they organise themselves in space are the story and the time and the climate and the characters of the production. We notice that emotion occupies and changes the whole person. And if we practise watching plays just a little bit we see that the angle someone cuts as they move upstage at a particular moment in the drama might touch us very powerfully; or that a man trying not to fall has a metaphorical as well as a literal meaning. These are often the things that remain with us: things about the body, things about its relationship with space. Wonderful things.

And it's the same with the voice, with speech. We really listen in the theatre in the same way we really look. Theatres are big buildings – large rooms – they give the voice time to be heard. So that even (sometimes especially) in the cheap seats we hear the full sound of the performer resonating with the materials of the building we are in. We notice and respond (or fail to respond) to an actor's whole voice, way beyond its ability to carry mere information. We listen to its range, to the notes within the voice, its dimensions and harmonics, its qualities: we hear the way it moves. We can tell when a thought has really dropped through the breath to hit off a word in the actor's gut that connects out to us in the audience, or to something that's happened in our world that day: we hear when they're telling the truth. These moments can make an audience of several hundred collectively shudder or laugh.

We hear too and notice how crucial rhythm and timing are – how they relate to listening and playfulness. We notice that sharing the music of language is a game more sensuous than anything that can be captured by a photograph.

It requires no special knowledge to see and hear these things. Everybody sees and hears them.

Many people just call them acting: good acting/bad acting.

It does, however, require special knowledge to coach them and a knowledge, moreover, which has been grown through more than one lifetime. Which is why the best teachers are connected to other teachers: the material of theatre training is too simple not to need a collective intelligence to understand how to share it.

Without consistent and particular work on these two areas, on voice and on movement, led by teachers of calibre such as Jackie Snow, it's hard for most actors to manage early on. It's hard to get going. And once the actor does get started they will need a strong technical facility to grow and develop. To sustain a career; to realise their potential; to mature and age – to be a good artist.

And this is why drama schools and theatres have specialists who know how to work in these fields, how to teach exercises and give notes and set work that foregrounds some of the definable parts of the craft of acting. It's why we're paid to watch and listen.

But what I find particularly interesting is that the more time I spend teaching, the more I realise that good voice and movement work really are one thing, and part of an extended trinity with the teachable techniques of acting. Technical actor training doesn't just lead to acting – it doesn't provide tools – it is the thing itself. Three things that are one thing: one thing which is three. A little pedagogical mystery all of our own.

And yet it's not so mysterious if we look at how an excellent teacher like Jackie Snow, teaching from the systems she has studied, trains actors.

How movement helps voice. Nowhere is the connection more clear and fundamental between the body and the voice than through the medium of the breath: for the voice is breath and it's the whole body that breathes, or fails to.

And yet some types of movement encourage holding the breath on an action; or breathing in particular ways which control an impulse, or are empty of thought – these are not good for an actor. Others systems might encourage the body to move in a way that will inhibit the centring of weight that will let the breath drop in fully; or organise the body around an aesthetic which inhibits the taking of whatever breath the moment demands – the breath that responds to what it hears: to listening. Jackie understands all this from an acting perspective and all her work encourages and develops the right breath for an actor.

Another example is in the relationship between tension and balance in the whole body and the actor's ability to find space for sound in the throat and mouth. For without a degree of freedom and poise between the body and the head, the channel through which the voice moves, cannot release in the right way and tensions will enter into the system to compensate. These tensions will cut out elements of the voice's resonance and interfere with clear articulation. Some of these tensions are surprising – every voice teacher knows that tight thumbs relate to binding in the root of the tongue.

This is all true of the body in space, that part of a technical training which is sometimes called alignment or, perhaps more traditionally, posture. With consistency and repetition the work in this book will help you open and free the body to find its length and weight and flexibility, which will enable you to accept the specific breathing, resonance and articulation work you will encounter in other classes.

All of which will help you secure and free your voice.

As well as this work, which carefully unpicks tension in the body, Jackie's work develops potential through movement – it extends the actor's physical understanding of herself from the habitual to the possible. As you develop an extended vocabulary of the ways you can use yourself in motion, you may discover, if you allow it, that the same can happen to your sound.

There can be linguistic benefits from movement work too, for exercises which explore rhythm and dimension in space are close to dance and music, both of which enter into language. So that if you can apply the lessons these exercises might help you find the arc of a phrase of formal prose in a restoration comedy – its line. This is only true of the right kind of training. Pilates, ballet, running, Bikram yoga and weight training may do all sorts of things to the body, some of which might be very useful to an actor and some of which are less so. But I don't think any of them will make you better at speaking Shakespeare. Jackie's work can.

Finally, and for me most crucially, Jackie's exercises tirelessly pursue the relationship between thought as an image – leading to an impulse – which becomes a truthful movement. Which is how the voice works too – from the simplicity of a single exclamation to the relatively complex gesture of a sentence, where a subject affects the object via the agency of a verb.

And this of course is the same as playing an action: it is playing well. It's good acting.

The work in this book is excellent work and it comes from a superb teacher via a deeply considered tradition of movement training. I know Jackie Snow well, and I trust her completely.

So, if you want to become a better actor; if you want to have a better voice: do these exercises.

And then do them again.

Robert Price
Senior Voice Tutor
RADA

Example classes (DVD: Exercise 34)

The following classes are about one and a half hours long.

Class 1

This class can be done early on in the training, or revisited at different times during training. There is often a need to revisit the early work, and if on a three year course, this is especially true when students are late into their second year and are full of trepidation for the imminent arrival of the theatre and their final year.

Concentrating on the breath, focusing on the weight and release, and revisiting exercises they learnt in the first year, which after six terms of training, they tend to do in a much different fashion than they did when they first learnt it – it is the process of rediscovering.

1. Run if ... you had a good Easter, bad Easter, like Chinese food, love maths, like Indian food, if you cooked for someone etc. Beat the drum and when it stops, everyone halts and plants their feet and floats up through the spine.
2. Then run and hold hands with someone you have never done movement with.
3. Walk with them and enjoy looking at them.
4. Tell each other what you are good at in movement terms and what you are not so good at.
5. Give each other a big cuddle.
6. Run with another person who you have not done movement with and this time stop and look at each other and tell the other person what you think they would be good at in movement just by looking at them.
7. Stop talking and one person stands (they can close their eyes if they want).
8. The other person explores their face, throat, neck and hair with their finger tips.

Teaching point
For people who find this too difficult, persevere for a little while so the person can benefit, but if it is too uncomfortable, ask them to shut their eyes then massage down the spine with their fingers as they roll through the spine down to the bottom, knees released and bottom up in the air.

9. Pat the body and ribs and shake out the torso and neck and then build back up through the spine until the whole posture is realised.
10. Loosen the arms and move them around in their sockets and joints making sure they are free.
11. Pat down the body massaging the calves and the thighs.
12. Get a mat out and in twos.
13. One person lies on their back with their eyes closed or open as they prefer.

14. The other person sits at their head and takes the head in one hand, feel the weight and with the other hand massages the back of their neck and then move the head around in its socket.
15. Move the right arm around, again feeling the weight of the arm and the looseness of the joints.
16. Gently pull the arm out of its socket, unlocking the jaw as it goes.
17. Massage the hand, the forearm and bicep.
18. Move to the other arm and repeat.
19. Push both arms under the scapular and then massage between the scapular.
20. Move to the legs and massage the big fleshy parts, before moving them around in the joints.
21. Bend the right leg in and push it up to the right shoulder and stretch on a release.
22. Point the toes but don't push that point but keep the leg in the same position.
23. Release and push down again (the leg is much more durable than you think).
24. Then release it back down onto the floor.
25. Stretch the leg fully for the other person but be more careful in this position because it could hurt more easily.
26. Both partners roll over into folded leaf.
27. Breathe deeply in and out of the nose (five times is good), really filling the back of the rib cage.
28. Tuck the toes under into jack knife, bending the knees and releasing into the backs of the legs.
29. Indian push through.
30 Jack knife.
31. Uncurl through the spine and finding the length and breadth of the spine and the roots into the ground; unlock the knees and check out where the voice and breath is.
32. Walk and feel how you are rooted and free, and your voice is right down in the body.
33. Notice how the person who hasn't been 'done'. how they don't feel as centred and rooted.
34. Swap over and again from the folded leaf onwards make sure both people do it so that they can see that it stays in the body.
35. To end the class, let everybody lie flat on their back for two minutes, palms facing the ceiling and semi or full supine.
36. Everybody flops over onto their tummies and roll into folded leaf, tuck the toes under and roll up through the spine. Walk in the space, checking the breath, voice and body.

Class 2

When the students have mastered the full torso swing or even if they are still learning it, this class is useful to embed it into their bodies in an integral and holistic way, with acting and voice.

1. Run and stop in a space. The students should think about filling the room, so that they are all evenly spread through the space.
2. Shake down the whole of the torso to the floor.
3. Uncurl up through the spine.
4. Repeat, building on the quality of the run, i.e. running through the feet and swinging the arms freely by your sides.

5. Build on the awareness of yourself in the space.

6. Be aware of how to stop with alertness and freedom, floating and release. Note: every time you drop and roll up through your spine, you should feel more connection with the legs and more freedom in the spine neck and head.

7. Repeat and stand and face someone and then uncurl through the spine and really see the other person as if you were about to speak to them.

8. Turn and face the front and chew and stretch through all of the body as if you are waking up.

9. Rib stretches up, side and forward (about eight on each side and in each position, but it normally depends on the time of day as to how many you do) (see rib stretches, p. 47).

10. Shake down through the spine (see shake downs, p. 50).
    The number of shake downs done will depend on how advanced the class or the students are. So for example:
    ○ 8 knees, 8 just the head, 8 upper spine, 8 middle spine, 8 down to the floor.
    ○ Then on 4s, 2s, and 1s.
    ○ Shake downs to the right side and the left side.
    Again depending on the level of the class:
    ○ Arm swing 8 straight and 8 looking under twice through.
    ○ Pelvic rocks
    ○ Leg swings 16 on either leg.
    ○ Stretching the feet (see footwork, p. 29), i.e. push to the ball of the foot stretch push and lower.

11. ⦿ Run and stop in the space, well balanced through the feet, and the legs and spine floating up (DVD: Exercise 35).

12. Take the arms up the front of the body.

13. Heavy dropped full torso swing.

14. Rise onto the toes and, taking the arms up from the sides, lengthen the back and lower.

15. Repeat facing someone who is a good distance away from you.

16. Again with someone else a long way away from you.

17. And again but with someone near to you.

18. Discuss the different effects it has on you.
    Usually when the person is medium distance apart it feels as if they are having a general conversation. Close, it's as if they are having a more intimate conversation and far apart it's as if they are trying to tell somebody something over a crowded room.

19. Do it with men only and women standing arms down and receptive to how it feels.
    It is different if it is done far away or near or two men on one women, etc. It has a real courtly feel to it, Greek tragedy, or even just reverence to the other person.

20. After you have talked about it, do the exercise with the men standing still, the women running and stopping in front of them. Again try one on one, near distance, far distance and two on one and three on one, etc.

21. Talk about how that feels. There are always strong opinions on this one!

22. Everyone lies down on the floor and lets everything fall into the floor.

23. Flop over on your tummy and bring the legs underneath you and uncurl up through the spine.

24. Once more and this time with a line of text to each other on the rise and lower, making sure the line of text coincides with the movement of the arms.
25. Make sure the spine is lengthened and the ribs are full of air.

Finish the class by one last run in the space, stand and full torso swing, rise and lower incorporating the whole class.

Class 3

This is a class for a new group of students. It has plenty of games, which means the students learn how to play with each other, and build up trust and begin to generally free the body; it makes them less self-conscious with one another.

The space work allows them to begin to be more aware of themselves in their surroundings and the individual pure movement work allows them to begin the process of freeing and strengthening the body for it to become ultimately more articulate in transformation; the blind lead and falling into each other encourages trust.

Game section
1. Name game (see p. 4–5).
2. Cat and mouse (see p. 5).
3. Ships and shores (see p. 6).
4. Music game (see p. 7).
5. Walking in space (see p. 15).
6. Touching finger tips exercise (see p. 17).

Pure movement section
1. Standing on own in space facing the front (see p. 24).
2. Chew and yawn and stretch the body (see p. 33).
3. Stand on mountain and feel the roots (see p. 24).
4. Rib stretches (see p. 47).
5. Shake downs (see p. 50).
6. ⊛ Working down through the spine in pairs (DVD: Exercise 36).
7. Lie on floor relax into gravity for two minutes (see p. 112).
8. Semi supine and clock face exercise (see p. 42).
9. Slow arms for 40 counts (see p. 35).
10. Roll over into folded leaf (see p. 73).
11. Uncurl through the spine (remembering the partners fingers) (see p. 36).

Trust section
1. Blind lead (see p. 113).
2. Falling into each others arms (see p. 114).
3. Finish holding hands in a circle and discuss how it went.

Class 4

Once the students have begun to master all the swings, then it is exhilarating and freeing to do a swing based class such as this.

1. Run and stop in the space (several times, working on the run with intention and the stopping without tension).
2. Chewing through the body.
3. Rib stretches, 8 up, 8 side, 8 forward.
4. Shake downs through the spine (8, 4, 2, 1).
5. Bow and arrow arm swing (16 on each arm).
6. Arm swing travelling across the room (swing on the spot four times and then travel by galloping to the other side of the room four times and repeat on the spot and repeat the travelling as many times as the space allows.
7. Peeping under swing.
8. Peeping under swing travelling across the room (as 6).
9. Figure of eight arm swing.
10. Figure of eight swing travelling across the room (as 6).
11. Leg swings.
12. Robert Redford swings (8).
13. Full torso swings (8).
14. ☉ Linking the movements together (DVD: Exercise 37).
    ○ Big squat.
    ○ Come up through an arched spine (1 and 2 and 3 and 4).
    ○ Lateral body swing.
    ○ Staying down there (1 and 2 and 3 and swing up on 4, stay there opening arms out to the side 5, 6).
    ○ Repeat three times and then drag the right leg to the left leg in parallel, lengthening the spine, taking the arms over the head, one big full torso swing and rise and over.
    ○ Repeat the exercise opposite a partner.
15. Lie down on the floor, supine or semi supine, for the body to relax and centre.

Class 5

Cat class: a strengthening and stretching, one and a half hours

1. Ships and shores (see p. 6).
2. Music game (see p. 7).
3. Rib stretches (8 up, 8 side, 8 forward) (see p. 47).
4. Shake downs or bounces (8, 4, 2, 1 (see p. 50).
5. Bow and arrow arm swing (8 on each arm) (see p. 54).

6. Figure of eight arms swing (8 on each arm) (see p. 55).
7. Leg swings (16 on each leg) (see p. 61).
8. Lateral body swings (8) (see p. 58).
9. Full torso swings, rise and lower (see p. 59).

Link movements together. This is to build the strength, suppleness, and release and body articulation through continuation and flow.

Move across the floor in lines of four.

- ○ Four leg swings with the right leg (1 and 2 and 3 and 4).
- ○ Swing the right leg behind in a long lunge (5, 6, 7 and 8).
- ○ Bring the left leg back to meet the right leg in a jack knife (hold the position (1, 2, 3, 4).
- ○ Indian push through (5, 6).
- ○ Pull back into jack knife (7, 8).
- ○ Walk the hands to meet the feet. Unlock the knees (1, 2,3, 4).
- ○ Full torso swing, rise and lower (5, 6, 7 and 8).
- ○ Repeat four times.

Each time change number iv. for another of the Cat movements which need practice, i.e. leg kick, hip roll, pounce and pike.

10. Put the mats out and everyone lies on their tummies.
11. Do The Cat from beginning to end with the intention of being a cat.
12. Facing a partner, do part of The Cat with a pre-decided dramatic intention.
13. Perform it in two groups, with one group watching the other and guessing what the intention is.

Class 6

Pure movement into an acrobatic class

1. Ships and shores (see p. 6).
2. Music game (see p. 7).
3. Rib stretches (8 up, 8 side, 8 forward) (see p. 47).
4. Shake downs or bounces (8, 4, 2, 1) (see p. 50).
5. Bow and arrow arm swing (8 on each arm) (see p. 54).
6. Figure of eight arms swing (8 on each arm) (see p. 55).
7. Leg swings (16 on each leg) (see p. 61).
8. Lateral body swings (8) (see p. 58).
9. Full torso swings, rise and lower (see p. 59).
10. The Cat (see p. 66).

Big stretches with partners (see p. 90)

i. Partner A sits on the floor (feet together). Partner B places their bottom (**very carefully**) at the base of A's back and then fold the spines together. A flops down over their feet and B lies carefully over the top of them. Stay for one minute, before carefully coming up, bodies together. Swap.

ii. Repeat exercise with the legs together, outstretched in front.

    iii. Repeat exercise with the legs wide apart.

    iv. Standing back to back; partner A lifts partner B over their back, bending their knees and placing their elbows on their knees for back protection. Swap.

    v. Repeat falling into each other front to back.

11. Put the mats in to three long lines.

    i. Forward roll to lie.

    ii. Forward roll to squat.

    iii. Forward roll, high jump, forward roll, star jump, forward roll, tuck and tuck and tuck and tuck, jump.

    iv. Side roll.

    v. Side roll into forward roll to lie into side roll.

    vi. Backward roll.

    vii. Backward roll to straddle.

    viii. Backward roll to straight legs.

    ix. Cartwheels on both sides.

    x. Cartwheels to side roll to cartwheels.

    xi. One handed cartwheels.

    xii. Arab springs.

Partner work

i. Flying angels.

ii. Standing on backs.

iii. Chest stands on backs.

iv. Back bend over each other into handstand and down onto the feet.

v. Sitting on shoulders.

vi. Standing on shoulders.

Class 7

This is a floor exercise for loosening the limbs and the spine, using gravity and relaxation

1. Place the mats around the room and turn down the lights.

2. Everybody lies on a mat, palms facing the ceiling and legs two feet apart.

3. With meditation music, talk through the relaxation (see p. 112) (twenty minutes).

4. Tuck the hands underneath the hips and move the head gently and heavily from side to side as if saying no. Nod it up and down gently as if saying yes. Move it in a circular motion, clockwise and anti-clockwise (16 times very slowly each movement).

5. Slide the arms above the head along the floor in a semi-circular shape (like a child playing angels in the snow), five times up and down.

6. Place the arms right angles to the body. For 40 slow counts raise the arms smoothly in front of you until the palms are facing each other. Lift the arms up and down, in and out of their sockets. Turn the palms

to face the front and for 40 counts, smoothly take the arms over the head. Bring them back up for 40 and back out for 40.

7. Bring the knees on the chest and move the legs in their sockets like two spoons in a basin of mayonnaise.

8. Take both legs over to the right arm pit and look along the left arm. Sweep the left arm over the head until you are in the foetal position. Repeat this movement five times, encouraging the shoulders to open to the floor.

9. Place the feet back onto the floor and do the clock face exercise (see p. 42).

10. Roll over into folded leaf. Tuck the toes under and roll up through the spine into the neutral stance. Take it into a walk around the room, waking up and noticing the difference in the body.

Class 8

This is a floor class in groups of three,

1. Have one mat between three people.
2. A lies on their back. B sits at their head and C at their feet.
3. B holds the head as C holds the feet. They pull A's body in two directions. Release. Repeat 4 times.
4. B takes one arm and C takes the other. Move the arm carefully in around holding the hand and under the elbow. Make sure A has no tension in their arms. B and C hold A's hand and pulls the arms up to the ceiling as if they are being pulled out of the sockets and drops them back in again. Slowly stretch the arms over A's head. B holds down the arms whilst C goes to the legs and swings the legs from side to side (jelly wobble).
5. B takes one leg and C takes the other.
6. B and C take one each of A's hand under the knee and the other holds the ankle or the foot.
7. Move the leg loosely in its socket, in the same way as the arm.
8. Place the legs back down and B massages A at the back of the neck and face, while C massages A's legs.
9. Flip A over onto their front.
10. B and C take a shoulder each and lifts A's torso off the ground and then lowers gently (be careful not to compress the spine).
11. B and C lift the legs off the floor, pulling them away from the torso, so that again they are not compressing the spine.
12. C takes the feet and jelly wobbles the legs, while B keeps the shoulders down.
13. B massages the torso and head while C massages the legs.
14. A flops into folded leaf, and uncurls through the spine, noticing the differences in the body and the stance. Walk around the space to feel the difference.
15. Repeat the whole process with B and C.
16. Everybody lies down for five minutes to be able to revisit the release found then every body flop into folded leaf and uncurl up through the spine.

A note on Trish Arnold

Trish started her career training as a dancer at the Sadler's Wells Royal Ballet School. She went on to dance professionally with the Royal Ballet Company amongst others. After marrying and having two children, Trish began teaching ballet but came increasingly bored with this classical style of dance. Through friends she met a German dancer called Sigurd Leeder who at ran the Modern Dance Studio in London. Sigurd Leeder had worked closely with Kurt Joss in his ballet company; most famously creating the piece of work *The Green Table* (choreographed by Kurt Joss[4]).

Trish Arnold joined Sigurd Leeder and his company in London for two years and it was here that her work progressed from classical ballet to the more modern forms of movement. Sigurd Leeder's work centred on swings and space, with very quick footed movements. Trish found herself enamoured by Leeder's work; his use of swings and dimensions in space became an integral part of her future. The influence that Rudolph Laban's work had on both Kurt Joss and Sigurd Leeder's movement, based on the dynamics of space and weight, also showed itself clearly in Trish Arnold's practices.

In 1955, Trish Arnold accepted an offer to teach movement on the acting course at the LAMDA. She joined the principal Michael McOwen, vice principal Norman Ayrton and the remarkable voice teacher, Iris Warren, all of whom were extremely influential in Trish Arnold's development as an expert in the field of movement.

Trish describes herself as 'having been greatly influenced by the powerful voice coach, Iris Warren', she had a huge impact on all her ideas on movement, most importantly the vast difference between the needs of an actor and a dancer. When she arrived at LAMDA, Trish remembers Iris Warren: 'The first time I met her she rose to her full height and said: "And I hope you are not going to do anything which stops them breathing."'

The first lesson in training actors in movement!

It was during those early years at LAMDA that she began to learn the art of training actors in movement and to discover her passion for the importance of the body, breath and voice.

It was also at LAMDA that Trish Arnold became aware of the French teacher and director, Michel St Denis. Michael Mac Owen and Norman Ayrton had both worked with him and were very much moved to continue his unique and revolutionary style of actor training. Michael St Denis had inspired many during his time at the London Mask Theatre before the Second World War and afterwards at the Old Vic School in his employment of actor training involving movement, improvisation and mask work. It is these eclectic sources,

---

[4] Kurt Joss revolutionised ballet with his use of space and extension. He represented the more lyrical side of the modern ballet techniques that were developing in Germany and Austria, (in contrast to Mary Wigman, whose heavier, more earthy work influenced Martha Graham and the development of Modern dance in the United States).

the German influences of Sigurd Leeder , Litz Pisk and Martha Graham, wedded with the French Michael St Denis and his actor training, that has essentially shaped Trish Arnold's philosophies on movement training for actors and resulted in her position as Head of Movement at LAMDA from 1963–1974

During this period Trish furthered her own studies by becoming involved with the work of Jacques Le Coq in Paris. She ventured into movement coaching with professional actors on various productions with the English Stage Society under the direction of Bill Gaskill and Peter Gill. From 1967–1974 she also worked as a movement coach at the Stratford Ontario Festival in Canada and in 1968 worked for a short while at the New York University as a movement teacher. It was in Stratford, Ontario that Trish Arnold began a close working relationship with the voice coach Kristin Linklater that was to last for many years. Michael Mac Owen would introduce them as 'Kristin Linklater, the voice, and Trish Arnold, the body.'

Kristin Linklater's work complemented very well with Trish Arnold's; Kristin called the work at Stratford 'band-aid stuff, patching and repairing actors' and this led to a greater need for the voice and movement work to integrate. Iris used to say: 'There is a breath with every movement – you don't hold your breath to do a movement, you let your voice go out with a movement .'

After Trish retired from LAMDA, Sue Lefton, who was heading the movement department at the Guildhall School of Music and Drama, asked her to join the team at Guildhall to introduce the pure movement work, which, from her own experience of her training with Litz Pisk, she felt was vital to the students' training. She then built the team, which included Wendy Allnutt who had also been trained by Litz (to teach animal study) and Jackie Snow, to train in movement for actors. This led to the philosophy of the work to be carried forward into the present and future. Jane Gibson, who had also trained with Litz and Trish, kept the philosophy of the training going at LAMDA.

Twenty years later, the training continues, in many drama schools.

All the teachers continue to have discussions and classes and tea with Trish, where at the age of 93, she continues to be as excited about the work as ever.

Further reading

Tea with Trish (DVD; Merry Conway)

The Actor and his Body (Litz Pisk, Methuen Drama, London, 1998)

Laban for Actors and Dancers (Jean Newlove, Nick Hern, London, 1993)

The Moving Body (Jacques Lecoq, Methuen Drama, London, 2001)

Towards a Poor Theatre (Jerzi Growtoski, Methuen Drama, London, 2002)

Michael Chekhov on Theatre and the Art of Acting (Mala Powers, Applause Theatre Books, New York, 2005)

May I Have the Pleasure (Belinda Quirey, Dance Books Ltd, Alton, 2008)

Index